# iN GUIDE PARIS

# PARIS

Few other cities have had as many songs written about them, have been used as a setting for films, novels, or plays as Paris – the city of lights, the city of love. The French capital enchants its visitors – often it is love at first sight. Whether you are enjoying a pastis in one of the street cafés in the buzzing Quartier Latin or a cruise on the River Seine, whether you are strolling through the Jardin du Luxembourg or immersing yourself in a work of art in one of the many museums – it is hard to resist the charms of this city.

From the first small settlement on the Île de la Cité, a vast urban area has developed over the centuries. Its many districts, however, can still be explored on foot today. And when your feet really won't carry you any longer, there's always the Métro – allegedly there's no point in Paris further than 500m (547 yds) away from a station.

# ABOUT THIS BOOK

*InGuide Paris* is illustrated with the stunning photographs you would expect to find in a large coffee-table book yet it is also a highly informative travel guide. District by district, inspiring images and vivid descriptions introduce all the sights, revealing many amazing facts about the city and its people, about art and culture, about the everyday and the unusual. In "Compact Paris", insider tips point out the best restaurants, hotels, and shops, as well as trendy neighborhoods, important addresses, and useful facts. Another chapter introduces the top museums in detailed descriptions and photographs. Finally, the City Walks are packed with shopping and dining tips that will inspire you to explore all of the Paris districts and areas. A detailed, removable city map completes this unique picture travel guide. It makes it easy for you to find all the city's highlights by grid reference.

| ÎLE DE LA CITÉ, RIVE DROITE | 8 | La Madeleine | 48 | Sorbonne | 96 |
|---|---|---|---|---|---|
| | | Fauchon | 50 | Panthéon | 98 |
| Ile Saint-Louis and Ile de la Cité | 10 | Place Vendôme | 52 | Clovis I | 100 |
| | | Gold and Jewels | 54 | Jardin du Luxembourg | 102 |
| Notre-Dame | 12 | Opéra Garnier | 56 | Palais du Luxembourg | 104 |
| Sainte-Chapelle, Conciergerie | 14 | Palais de la Bourse | 58 | Institut du Monde Arabe, Mosqueé de Paris | 106 |
| | | Palais Royal | 60 | | |
| Louvre | 16 | Forum des Halles | 62 | Musée d'Orsay | 108 |
| Masterpieces of the Louvre | 18 | Centre Pompidou | 64 | Impressionists | 110 |
| Tuileries | 20 | Hôtel de Ville | 66 | Pioneers of modern art | 112 |
| Place de la Concorde | 22 | Marais | 68 | River Seine | 114 |
| Champs-Elysées, Arc de Triomphe | 24 | Place des Vosges | 70 | Markets | 116 |
| | | Victor Hugo | 72 | | |
| French Film | 26 | Michelin-starred restaurants | 74 | FAUBOURG SAINT-GERMAIN | 118 |
| Pont Alexandre III, Grand Palais, Petit Palais | 28 | Place de la Bastille, Opéra Bastille | 76 | Palais Bourbon | 120 |
| World Exhibitions | 30 | Storming of the Bastille | 78 | Musée Rodin | 122 |
| Palais de Chaillot, Jardins de Trocadéro | 32 | The French Revolution | 80 | Hôtel and Dôme des Invalides | 124 |
| | | Musée National Picasso | 82 | | |
| Elysée Palace, Faubourg Saint-Honoré | 34 | Palaces of the Noblity | 84 | Napoleon Bonaparte | 126 |
| | | Musée des Arts et Métiers | 86 | Montparnasse Cemetery | 128 |
| Baron Haussmann and the Transformation of Paris | 36 | | | Le Bistro | 130 |
| | | RIVE GAUCHE, QUARTIER LATIN | 88 | Eiffel Tower | 132 |
| Grands Boulevards | 38 | | | Gustave Eiffel | 134 |
| Printemps | 40 | Saint-Germain-des-Prés | 90 | Musée du Quai Branly | 136 |
| Fashion | 42 | Jean-Paul Sartre and Simone de Beauvoir | 92 | Palais de Tokyo | 138 |
| Galeries Lafayette | 44 | | | Liberty Statue, Île des Cygnes | 140 |
| Métro | 46 | Chansons | 94 | | |

6   **Paris**

# CONTENTS

Left: Visitors enter one of the most important museums in the world via the Glass Pyramid in the courtyard of the Louvre; previous pages: The Notre-Dame Cathedral on the Île de la Cité and the Sacré-Cœur Basilica on the hill of Montmartre.

| | |
|---|---|
| **FURTHER AFIELD** | 142 |
| Bois de Boulogne | 144 |
| The stations of Paris | 146 |
| La Défense | 148 |
| Sacré-Coeur | 150 |
| Montmartre | 152 |
| Pariser Nightlife | 154 |
| Henri de Toulouse-Lautrec | 156 |
| Canal Saint-Martin | 158 |
| Père-Lachaise Cemetery | 160 |
| Edith Piaf | 162 |
| Parc de la Villette | 164 |
| National Library | 166 |
| Mitterrand and his buildings | 168 |
| | |
| **BEYOND PARIS** | 170 |
| Versailles | 172 |
| Louis XIV | 174 |
| André Le Nôtre | 176 |
| Malmaison | 178 |
| Basilica of Saint-Denis | 180 |
| Disneyland Paris | 182 |
| Fontainebleau | 184 |

| | |
|---|---|
| **COMPACT PARIS** | 186 |
| Île de la Cité, Rive Droite | 188 |
| Rive Gauche, Quartier Latin | 196 |
| Faubourg Saint-Germain | 204 |
| Further afield | 208 |
| Beyond Paris | 212 |
| | |
| **MAJOR MUSEUMS** | 216 |
| Louvre | 218 |
| Musée National du Moyen Age – Musée de Cluny | 222 |
| Musée National Picasso | 226 |
| Centre Pompidou – Musée National d'Art Moderne | 230 |
| | |
| **CITY WALKS** | 234 |
| Île de la Cité, Rive Droite | 236 |
| Rive Gauche, Quartier Latin | 240 |
| Faubourg Saint-Germain | 244 |
| Seine Cruise | 248 |
| | |
| **APPENDIX** | 252 |
| Index | 252 |
| Picture credits | 256 |
| Imprint | 256 |

Paris 7

The view extends from the Pompidou Centre across the inner city in this stunning evening scene. The Gothic Tour of Saint-Jacques rises majestically in the background.

# ÎLE DE LA CITÉ, RIVE DROITE

Two islands in the River Seine, the Île de la Cité and Île Saint-Louis, form the heart of Paris. The Celtic Parisii settled here in about 300 BC, and the Romans, too, established themselves on the islands. With the construction of Notre-Dame and a royal palace, the Île de la Cité became the focal point of both religious and political power in the Middle Ages. Today, the government offices are located on the Right Bank (Rive Droite), where the French president holds court in the Élysée Palace and where, on the Champs-Élysées, many elegant boutiques highlight the wealth and purchasing power of their well-heeled customers.

Paris 9

# ÎLE DE LA CITÉ, RIVE DROITE

Originally, there were three islands on the River Seine, which flows through the heart of Paris. In 1614, the two smaller islands – the Île aux Vaches and the Île Notre-Dame – were linked together, and in 1725 the resulting single island was renamed Saint-Louis. While the Île de la Cité attracts visitors thanks to its important historic monuments, people go to the Île Saint-Louis simply to wander through the quiet streets lined with 17th- and 18th-century palaces. In the mid-19th century, the poet Charles Baudelaire wrote his weighty volume of poetry *Les Fleurs du Mal* (*Flowers of Evil*) in the

10    Paris

# ILE SAINT-LOUIS AND ILE DE LA CITÉ

Hôtel de Lauzun. Even in more recent times, the Île Saint-Louis has boasted its share of famous residents, such as Georges Pompidou, the former state president who has been immortalized through his cultural complex, the actor, Jean-Claude Brialy, and the singer, Georges Moustaki.

The view of the top of the Île Saint-Louis, with the Cité and Notre-Dame cathedral in the background, is simply stunning (large picture top). The Pont Neuf, the oldest bridge in Paris (below), stretches across the western end of the Île de la Cité. Top: small shops line the alleys of the Île Saint-Louis.

Paris 11

# ÎLE DE LA CITÉ, RIVE DROITE

Notre-Dame – or, to be more precise, the square facing the main entrance to the cathedral – is not only the focal point of Paris, it is the geographical hub of the whole country. A metal plate set in the ground in front of the cathedral marks the spot from which every point in France is measured. Completed in 1345 (the foundation stone was laid by Bishop Maurice de Sully in 1163), the western façade of this Gothic building has a wealth of fascinating sculptures. Above the three carved portals, representing the life of the Virgin, the life of St Anne, and the Last Judgment, are figures in the

# NOTRE-DAME 2

Gallery of Kings. These are reproductions, as the originals were literally decapitated in the Revolution; a few of the heads are displayed in the Musée de Cluny. The interior, partially redesigned in the 18th century, has a solemn atmosphere, reinforced when the great organ is played.

Seen from the banks of the Seine, Notre-Dame cathedral, characterized by its Gothic style, dominates la Cité (large picture). Above: the baroque main altar in the church. Top: one of the magnificent rose windows.

Paris 13

# ÎLE DE LA CITÉ, RIVE DROITE

The high Gothic Sainte-Chapelle was built between 1245 and 1248 by King Louis IX (Saint Louis) to provide a suitable setting for the valuable relics that this famous crusader supposedly brought back to France – the Crown of Thorns and drops of the blood of Christ, a piece of the True Cross, and many more. The magnificent windows in the Upper Chapel, which bathe everything in a ghostly light, tell the story of these relics as well as the life of Jesus and other biblical stories. The Conciergerie is part of a medieval royal palace and was converted into a prison around 1400.

# SAINTE-CHAPELLE
# CONCIERGERIE

During the French Revolution, prisoners spent their last days here before being taken to the guillotine. Those prisoners included Marie Antoinette, Charlotte Corday, the murderess of the rebel Marat – and some of the Revolutionaries themselves, such as Georges Danton and Robespierre.

Servants heard mass in the simpler Lower Chapel (large picture), while the Upper Chapel with its filigree tracery and beautiful stained-glass windows (above) was reserved for the nobility. Top: View over the Seine toward the Conciergerie.

Paris 15

# ÎLE DE LA CITÉ, RIVE DROITE

Situated on the Right Bank of the Seine, the Louvre was originally commissioned by Philippe Auguste in 1200 as a fortress, remnants of which can still be seen. François I rebuilt the fortress and for a period the Louvre served as the residence of the French kings, who put their own stamp on it by adding extensions, such as thoseby Henri IV and Louis XIII. The Cour Carrée and its surrounding buildings were created under the rule of Louis XIV, while the emperors Napoleon I and Napoleon III contributed to the interior design of the present Louvre buildings. In 1981, under the aegis of

The Glass Pyramid designed by Ieoh Ming Pei is the focal point of the Louvre building complex. Pei had the equestrian statue of Louis XIV, conceived by Gianlorenzo Bernini, built at the same time as the pyramid (large picture).

# LOUVRE 5

François Mitterrand, the "Grand Louvre" project was launched, in order to expand the exhibition area. As part of the renovation work, Ieoh Ming Pei created an entrance to the halls with his spectacular Glass Pyramid (built in 1989), for the huge number of visitors who arrive each day.

The Louvre is one of the largest and most famous museums in the world and among the amazing wealth of artistic treasures on display, there are a few works that immediately spring to mind at the mention of the gallery. First in line is, of course, Leonardo da Vinci's *Mona Lisa*, whose sensational theft in 1911 has contributed as much to the mystique of this painting as her enigmatic smile. It is almost impossible to imagine the Louvre without other works, such as two Greek statues of classical beauty – the *Winged Victory of Samothrace* and the *Venus de Milo*. But there are many other masterpieces to be discovered – the Codex Hammurabi, a stone inscribed with one of the oldest collections of laws in the world is found in the Mesopotamian Collection; wonderful examples of sculptures, frescoes, and half-reliefs are in the Egyptian Collection as well and countless treasures

# MASTERPIECES OF THE LOUVRE

from ancient Greece and Italy. The Sculpture Collection provides an overview of French sculpture, and includes works such as *The Embarkation for Cythera* by Antoine Watteau, Eugène Delacroix's revolutionary painting, *Liberty Leading the People*, or the *Medici Cycle* by Peter Paul Rubens.

Everyone knows Jan Vermeer's painting *The Lacemaker* and, of course, Leonardo's *Mona Lisa*, but Watteau's *Gilles* is also worth seeing (top, from left). Large picture: the goddess of hunting, Diana, flanked by other ancient sculptures.

# ÎLE DE LA CITÉ, RIVE DROITE

Anyone mentioning the name Tuileries usually means the Jardin des Tuileries, for the Tuileries palace was destroyed in 1871 during the rebellion of the Paris Commune. Commissioned by Catherine de' Medici in the middle of the 16th century, the palace was the city residence for the kings for several centuries. Nowadays the gardens between Place de la Concorde and Louvre are a perfect spot for visitors to relax by the great Bassin, and to admire the beautiful sculptures by Aristide Maillol which are dotted around the gardens. There are two museums on the edges of the Tuileries. Near the

From the Arc de Triomphe du Carrousel, the eye drifts across the Tuileries and the gardens of the Louvre (top). An oasis in the heart of the busy city, close to the Louvre (large picture), it is easy to forget the heavy traffic on the freeway on the Seine bank as well as the major traffic hub of the Place de la Concorde a stone's throw away. In the Tuileries, the greenery and the bird song is a treat for the eyes and ears.

# TUILERIES

Rue de Rivoli stands the Jeu de Paume, once the museum of the Impressionists, and today an exhibition space for photographic and video art, while nearer the Seine is the Musée de l'Orangerie, where the *Nymphéas* (*Water-Lilies*), the famous painting by Claude Monet is the highlight.

# ÎLE DE LA CITÉ, RIVE DROITE

The Place de la Concorde looks back on a turbulent history. Originally laid out as a royal square it was renamed as Place de la Révolution in 1792. Over 1,000 people died here beneath the Revolutionary guillotine including King Louis XVI and his wife Marie Antoinette who were beheaded along with many others. When the worst abominations of the Revolution began to abate in 1795, the square was given its present name: the place of unity. In the middle stands the gold-tipped obelisk of Luxor which was given to the "citizen king" Louis-Philippe as a gift from the Egyptian

# PLACE DE LA CONCORDE

government. In each of the eight corners of the square stand statues that symbolize the French cities of Brest, Rouen, Lyon, Marseille, Bordeaux, Nantes, Strasbourg, and Lille. The northern end of the square is formed by two palaces housing the Hôtel de Crillon and France's marine ministry.

The magic of the elegant Place de la Concorde can only fully be appreciated at night, when the illuminated fountains create an enchanting setting.

# ÎLE DE LA CITÉ, RIVE DROITE

The Avenue des Champs-Élysées is one of the world's most famous streets. This is where the great military parade takes place each year on July 14, the French national holiday; it is also where spectators cheer on the cyclists to the finishing line in the punishing Tour de France and where Parisians and visitors from around the world welcome in the New Year. But even on normal days the stretch of road between the Place de la Concorde and Place Charles de Gaulle is busy with traffic and pedestrians. The Arc de Triomphe stands proudly in place, as cars whirl around it. A dozen roads radiate out from

At all times of day a never-ending stream of cars flows along the Champs-Élysées (large picture), yet it is a pleasant avenue to stroll along under the trees. On the Place Charles de Gaulle rises the Arc de Triomphe (top), which is just under 50 m (165 ft) tall.

# CHAMPS-ÉLYSÉES
# ARC DE TRIOMPHE

the central arch forming a star shape, which is why the square was called Place de l'Étoile until 1969. Completed in 1836, the arch is a memorial to the victories of Emperor Napoleon. In the shadow of this symbolic monument, the flame on the Tomb of the Unknown Soldier flickers in remembrance.

French film began in 1885 with the Lumière brothers, who made short feature films such as *L'Arroseur arrosé*. The French film industry soon developed, even during World War II, when masterpieces such as *Les Enfants du Paradis* (*The Children of Paradise*) were still being produced. A high point of French film production was at the end of the 1950s and start of the 1960s, when films by the Nouvelle Vague (New Wave) attracted worldwide attention. Technical innovations such as the development of more sensitive film enabled film crews to move out of the studios and onto the streets and thus capture a whole new atmosphere. The shooting location (and in France that was often Paris) frequently became the star of the film in its own right, or a major feature of it. The Antoine Doinel films by François Truffaut – the best known of which, *Les Quatre Cent Coups* (*The 400 Blows*) –

# FRENCH FILM

is a good example of the Nouvelle Vague. More recent films focusing on the French capital include *Les Amants du Pont Neuf* (*The Lovers on the Bridge*) by Léos Carax, and Jean-Pierre Jeunet's *Le Fabuleux Destin d'Amélie Poulain* (*Amélie*), and Cédric Klapisch's romantic comedy *Paris*.

The world of film in France was marked by great directors such as François Truffaut, Jean-Luc Godard, and Claude Chabrol (top, from left). International stars like Catherine Deneuve (above top) and Michel Piccoli (large picture) have had an ongoing presence on the silver screen around the world.

# ÎLE DE LA CITÉ, RIVE DROITE

The foundation stone for Pont Alexandre III was laid in 1896 by the Russian Czar Nicholas II, the son of Alexander III, after whom the bridge was named. This masterpiece of bridge-building, which crosses the river Seine in a wide, single span, was completed in time for the World Exhibition in 1900. The neoclassical Grand Palais and Petit Palais were also constructed for the World Exhibition, and they both echo the bridge design in their sumptuous ornamentation. The Grand Palais is host to ever-changing art exhibitions, often of international renown and attracting large crowds of

# PONT ALEXANDRE III [10]
## GRAND PALAIS, PETIT PALAIS [11]

people. It was renovated between 1995 and 2007 following damage to the glass roof. The Petit Palais, which has also undergone renovation, is home to the art collection belonging to the city of Paris, whose treasures include work by European artists such as Dürer, Rubens, and Rembrandt, among others.

The neo-baroque Pont Alexandre III glitters in the evening light (large picture). It meets the Avenue Winston Churchill, which runs between the Grand Palais (top) and the Petit Palais (portal shown above).

Paris 29

World Exhibitions took place in Paris in 1855, 1867, 1878, 1889, 1900, 1925, and 1937. At a time when television did not yet beam pictures from around the world into every living room, and long-distance travel was all but impossible, these exhibitions were an important source of information for ordinary people. They also were the impetus for architects to design innovative structures such as the Eiffel Tower (1889) and the Palais de Chaillot (1937), whose previous structure, the Arab-inspired Trocadéro, had also been built for a World Exhibition (1878). It's also fascinating to see

The Trocadéro (large picture) was built for the World Exhibition in 1878. Top right: The Palais de l'Industrie was established on Paris' first World Exhibition, in 1855. Above top: View of the World Exhibition grounds of 1867. Above bottom: The Rover Seine and the entrance gate to the Exposition in 1900.

30  Paris

# WORLD EXHIBITIONS

which everyday items were presented as revolutionary novelties: for example the espresso machine (1855), the refrigerator (1878), and a type of moving staircase (1900), the blueprint for today's escalators. Nowadays, exhibitions of this kind have almost gone out of fashion.

# ÎLE DE LA CITÉ, RIVE DROITE

The Palais de Chaillot was built for the World Exhibition in 1937 on the site of the Trocadéro, a fantastically exotic structure, which had originally been built for the World Exhibition in 1878. The palace houses a number of different museums. At the Musée de la Marine (Navy Museum) you can see ships' models, paintings, and documents relating to navigation The Musée des Monuments Français (Museum of French Monuments) show cases models and casts of famous French buildings; together with the Institut Français d'Architecture (French Institute of Architecture), it

The gardens of the Trocadéro (large picture) and the forecourt of the Palais de Chaillot (above) near the Seine are popular meeting points for both local people and visitors. The view across the river toward the Eiffel Tower is unbeatable; at night, especially, the tower glows in an almost surreal light. The lights of the Palais de Chaillot (top) illuminate the forecourt, a favorite haunt of skateboarders.

# PALAIS DE CHAILLOT 🔢
## JARDINS DE TROCADÉRO 🔢

forms part of the Cité de l'Architecture et du Patrimoine (City of Architecture and Heritage). Exhibits on anthropology and prehistory can be seen at the Musée de l'Homme (Museum of Man), while the ethnological collection was incorporated into the new Musée du Quai Branly in 2006.

# ÎLE DE LA CITÉ, RIVE DROITE

Given its name, the Élysée Palace is surprisingly not on the Champs-Élysées – its garden faces the splendid boulevard but the palace itself is located on the Rue du Faubourg Saint-Honoré. The Élysée was constructed at the start of the 18th century for the Count of Evreux and passed, via the Marquise de Pompadour, into the possession of the French kings and, later, the emperor, Napoleon. Today, it is the focus of power as the home of the president of France. While political events generally take place behind closed doors, nearby shop windows display the newest designer creations.

The shop windows of elegant boutiques attract passing shoppers in the Rue du Faubourg Saint-Honoré (top). Political power is at home here – President Nicolas Sarkozy has governed from the Élysée Palace since 2007 (large picture). Stylish state receptions are often hosted here (above).

# ÉLYSÉE PALACE 14
# FAUBOURG SAINT-HONORÉ 15

Many international haute-couture names are here: Karl Lagerfeld, Jeanne Lanvin, Pierre Cardin, LouisFéraud, Yves Saint-Laurent, Hermès. The boulevard is also home to the best-known concert hall in Paris, the Salle Pleyel, which has been renovated and its art deco elegance restored.

Of great importance for the development of Paris were the plans for a comprehensive modernization of the city that Emperor Napoleon III conceived and realized together with the then prefect of Paris, Georges Eugène Baron Haussmann (1809–1891). At that time Paris was still a largely medieval city in building style as well as layout. Napoleon III was also driven by strategic considerations: with wide, straight roads, potential rebels would have less chance of being protected in secret hide-outs and would make it easier to manoeuvre troops; many people still recalled the fighting on the barricades in the streets of Paris during the 1848 uprisings. The Grands Boulevards, the Rue de Rivoli, the area around the Opéra (the present-day Opéra Garnier), the roads leading to the Arc de Triomphe – they all are either the work of Haussmann or at least they show his unmistake-

Top left: Emperor Napoleon III; top right: Baron Georges Eugène Haussmann. Above: Creation of the Avenue de l'Opéra and the Rue Saint-Roch. Large picture: A map dating from 1864 clearly shows the boulevards and main roads of Paris.

36   Paris

# BARON HAUSSMANN AND THE TRANSFORMATION OF PARIS

able influence. The neoclassical houses, too, that today seem to us so typical of Parisian design, were not built until the mid- to late 19th century. Haussmann's far-sighted plans created a network of roads that are still largely able to cope with the ever-increasing traffic in a major world city.

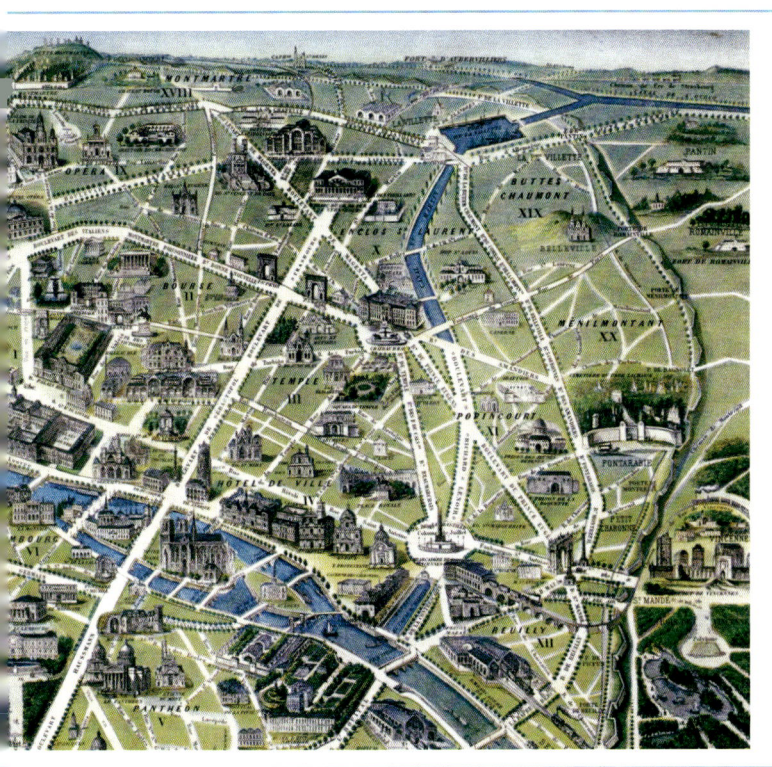

The construction of the grand boulevards began in the mid-19th century in accordance with the plans of Emperor Napoleon III. Georges-Eugène Haussmann, prefect of Paris from 1853 to 1870, played a significant part in the creation of these magnificent streets. The intention was to transform the medieval city to enable it to compete with its modern rivals, London and Berlin, as well as to have streets wide enough for troops and military transport in the event of popular unrest. To this end, generously proportioned avenues were created between Madeleine and Place de la République – the grand boulevards, instead of the earlier city fortifications from the time of Louis XIII. (The French word boulevard is related to the English word bulwark.) They include the Boulevards Beaumarchais, des Filles-du-Calvaire, du Temple, Saint-Martin, Saint-Denis, de Bonne Nouvelle, Poisson-

# GRANDS BOULEVARDS

ière, Montmartre, des Italiens, des Capucines, and de la Madeleine. While Avenue des Champs-Élysées is not a grand boulevard in the traditional sense, as it was in existence before the 19th century, it has transformed itself into one of the most famous and visited thoroughfares in the world.

The Boulevard des Capucines sits at right angles to the Avenue de l'Opéra at Garnier's opera house (large picture). From the air you can see how the avenues converge in a star shape on the Place Charles de Gaulle, formerly known as Place de l'Etoile (top). Dominating them is the 70-m-wide (230-ft) and nearly 2-km-long (1.2-mile) Champs-Élysées, which ends directly at the obelisk on the Place de la Concorde (above).

Paris 39

# ÎLE DE LA CITÉ, RIVE DROITE

Boulevard Haussmann boasts two of the largest department stores in Paris: Printemps and Galeries Lafayette. The Grand Magasin Printemps, opened in 1865, extends over four houses, two of which are located in the adjacent rue de Provence: Printemps de la Mode, Printemps de la Beauté et de la Maison (cosmetics, interior design, crockery), Printemps de l'Homme (men's fashion), and Citadium (designer fashion). There are also several up-scale eating establishments, ranging from cafés to elegant restaurants. Two of these feature special architectutal details: the Brasserie Printemps is

# PRINTEMPS 16

covered with a glazed art nouveau dome dating from 1924 and the Déli-cieux self-service restaurant (a word play: délicieux = delicious, cieux = heavens) on the roof of Level Nine, which offers its diners far-reaching panoramic views to Sacré-Coeur and the Eiffel Tower.

The magnificence of this mid-19th-century buildings also continues into the interior (large picture). But details such as the enchantingly beautiful stained-glass art nouveau cupola (above) are just the icing on the cake. Printemps is a temple to high-quality goods which appeal to all ages (top).

Paris 41

In spite of the increasing competition from London, Milan, and New York, Paris is still the focal point of haute couture today. This is where the term originated – even if it was an Englishman, Charles Frederick Worth, who founded the first house of haute couture in Paris in 1858. The rich and beautiful were willing to pay generously to be among his clientele. One of Worth's assistants, Paul Poiret, went on to become world famous for his fashionable designs. After World War II, haute couture opened up to wider sectors of the public through the New Look, created by Christian Dior, which was copied by many fashion companies. In the late 1940s, prêt-à-porter (ready-to-wear) clothes appeared on the scene and added a second string to the bows of many couture houses. Fashion was now available to a wider – but still affluent – clientele. To be considered part of Parisian haute couture,

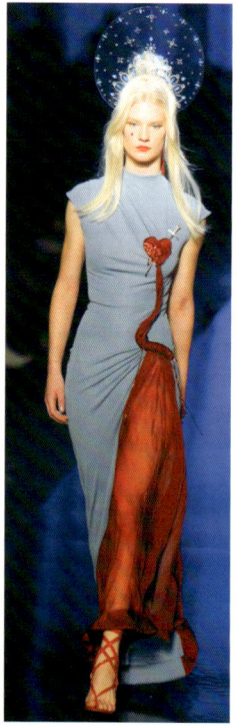

# FASHION

a couturier must present a collection twice a year comprising at least 35 "runs"; it must also have at least 25 full-time employees. The reputation of Paris as the world's fashion capital continues to be maintained by great names such as Chanel, Dior, Givenchy, Ungaro, Gaultier, Lacroix, and Valentino.

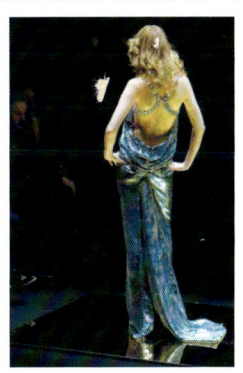

Paris, ever the byword for style and elegance, is probably still the main fashion show venue today. Creations by Chanel (top) and Georges Chakra (above) on the catwalk. Large pictures: fashion, relaxed or bold, presented here by Jean-Paul Gaultier (far left and left), Yves Saint-Laurent (middle and right) and Christian Lacroix (far right).

Paris

# ÎLE DE LA CITÉ, RIVE DROITE

The department store, Galeries Lafayette, boasts one of the best reputations in the world, and now has a number of branches in France and abroad, It opened its doors in 1894, almost 30 years later than its competitor, Printemps. The main branch has been located on the Boulevard Haussmann since 1912, in a magnificent building near the Havre-Caumartin métro station and only a stone's throw from the Palais Garnier. Much has changed over the course of time: whereas originally ladies' fashion dominated the scene, the range has been constantly broadened so that today men's

Particularly impressive is the several floors-high, superbly designed central sales hall in the Boulevard Haussmann, above which extends up to a beautiful stained-glass-adorned art nouveau dome. During the festive season, the Galeries Lafayette sparkles (top right), and a giant Christmas tree stands in the central hall.

44 Paris

# GALERIES LAFAYETTE 17

fashion as well as cosmetics, and toys, can all be found on a sales area of about 70,000 sq m (753,200 sq ft). The profile of its clientele has also changed. Among the 100,000 customers a day, Chinese visitors now form the main group of international shoppers, followed by the Americans, and Japanese.

Paris 45

The first metro lines entered service in 1900: line 1 from the Porte de Vincennes to Porte Maillot, line 2 from Étoile to the Trocadéro and Étoile to Porte Dauphine. Further lines were added in the next few years. These first metro lines were constructed under the supervision of the engineer Fulgence Marie Auguste Bienvenüe, after whom a metro station is named (Montparnasse-Bienvenüe). The elaborate art nouveau entrances to the stations were designed by French architect Hector Guimard. Today, many are still in existence such as at Porte Dauphine. The Paris network now comprises 16 lines with a total length of about 200 km (125 miles) with further expansion planned. In addition, there are five lines of the RER (Réseau Express Régional), a suburban railway that connects the capital with locations further afield such as Disneyland Paris and the air-

# MÉTRO

port at Roissy. Trains run between 5:00 and 0:30 and it is said that no point in Paris is more than 500 m (547 yards) from the nearest metro station. However, it is best to avoid the daily rush hours when commuters go to work in the morning or make their way back home in the evenings.

Many of the metro signs and station entrances today attest to the period around 1900 in when they were created, both in their design and the relatively narrow size of the stairs. This indicates how few passengers used the metro all those years ago.

Paris 47

# ÎLE DE LA CITÉ, RIVE DROITE

When you stroll down the Rue Royale, from the Place de la Concorde, you may be tempted to look twice. How did an ancient Greek temple end up in the middle of Paris? On the orders of Louis XV, a church topped by a dome, was planned for this site. But construction dragged on and was still a long way from completion when building work was interrupted by the Revolution. In 1806, Napoleon ordered new plans to be drawn for a temple of glory for his soldiers. He then changed his mind – the temple was to be a church after all. It was eventually dedicated in 1845, long after

The geometric shapes of the exterior (top) are contrasted by rounded forms in the interior, as the view through the main aisle into the altar space and the apse reveals (above). Even here, though, the columns with their Ionic chapters emphasize the reference back to the architectural details of classical antiquity. The main altar is adorned by a group of figures (large picture) created by the Italian sculptor Carlo Marochetti.

# LA MADELEINE 18

Napoleon's death. Ever since, the Madeleine has been the church of the local community. Its impressive interior was enriched by a superb organ in 1846, and in the second half of the 19th century two important composers were its titular or chief organists: Camille Saint-Saëns and Gabriel Fauré.

## ÎLE DE LA CITÉ, RIVE DROITE

For gourmets who prefer to dine at home, rather than in the Michelin-starred restaurants of the capital there is one top address in Paris: 24-26 place de la Madeleine, Paris 8ème. For more than a hundred years, this has been the home of Fauchon, the leading delicatessen in France, or perhaps in the entire world. Auguste Fauchon founded the company in 1886 and very quickly made it a great success thanks to the high-quality products on sale. From 1905, gourmets no longer had to travel to Paris in order to shop at Fauchon but could instead sit in the comfort of their

# FAUCHON 19

homes and choose their delicacies from a catalog that catered to their every need. However, with this method they missed out on sampling the delicacies such as those offered at the Salon de Thé in 1888. Today, you can visit the caviar bar at Place de la Madeleine for a true taste of luxury.

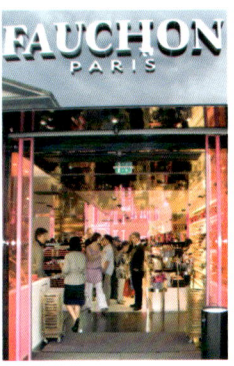

Fauchon, at the Place de la Madeleine (large picture) is a pilgrimage destination for food lovers from all over the world. The ambience (above) underlines the exclusivity of the delicatessen. In the 1960s it was here that the first selection of flavored black teas was created, but caviar (top) is the most popular delicacy.

Paris 51

# ÎLE DE LA CITÉ, RIVE DROITE

The Place Vendôme, commissioned as a royal square by Louis XIV and designed by the architect Jules Hardouin-Mansart, is now the haunt of the very rich. Many international names such as Cartier and Bulgari, give the square an air of exclusivity as does the Ritz, a luxury hotel ranking among the best in the world. Originally, an equestrian statue of Louis XIV stood in the middle of the square but this was toppled during the 1792 Revolution. From 1810, a column based on the beautiful Trajan's Column in Rome and crowned by a statue of Napoleon towered over the square. The original

# PLACE VENDÔME 20

column was destroyed during the Paris Commune's uprising. The artist Gustave Courbet, who was part of the rebellion, was sentenced to prison and told to pay for the restoration of the column, but fled the country. The column was rebuilt a few years later and now stands on the Place Vendôme.

Lit up at night (large picture and above) the Place Vendôme can transport you back into the past. The Ritz Hotel (top) is more than a hotel; it's an institution. Many famous people have stayed here – Hemingway celebrated the end of World War II at its bar. And the hotel was back in the headlines when Princess Diana set out from here on the journey that was to lead to her fatal accident.

Unless you are very rich, it's best just to go window-shopping in the Place Vendôme. Some of the most famous and expensive jewelers in the world have their stores here. For more than a hundred years, elegant jewelry and expensive watches have lured the lovers of beautiful and precious things to the harmoniously laid out square in the 1st Arrondissement. Jewelers of this class are known in France as the haute joaillierie, just as with haute-couture in fashion. In 1893 Frédéric Boucheron was the first of the great jewelers to settle in the Place Vendôme, and he was soon followed by Louis François Cartier (1898), Joseph Chaumet (1902), Alfred van Cleef & Solomon Arpels (1906), and in the 20th century by the exclusive shops of Fred, Mauboussin, and Bulgari; there are also the top-class watch brands such as Patek Philippe, Rolex, and Piaget. All the names are famous throughout

# GOLD AND JEWELS

the world. And if you wish to show off your expensive purchases within the appropriate context, you'll find the perfect opportunity to do so in the many bars and restaurants of the adjacent Ritz hotel. You can choose from the Hemingway or the Pool bar, or the very glitzy restaurant.

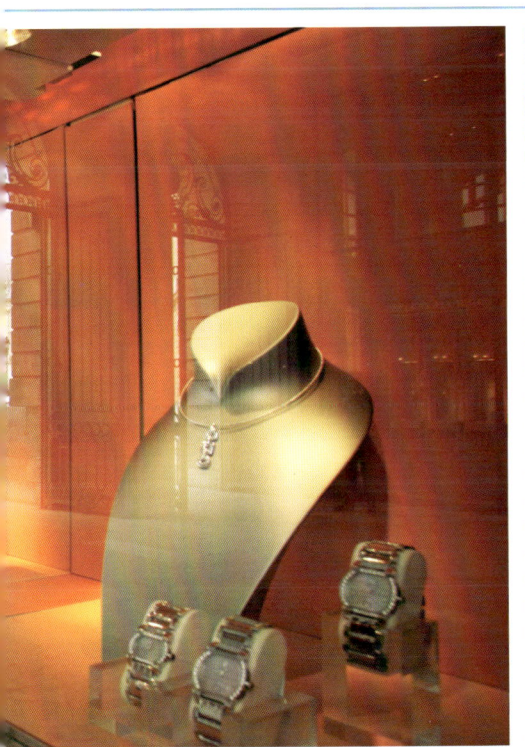

The oldest jeweler's store in the square is Boucheron (top), which was founded in 1858 and moved to its present headquarters on the Place Vendôme in 1893. Despite this long tradition everything here is modern – the late designer Alexander McQueen, created pieces for Boucheron. Fred (large picture and above), bearing the name of its founder, Fred Samuel, has enchanted its clients since the middle of the 19th century.

# ÎLE DE LA CITÉ, RIVE DROITE

Commissioned by Napoleon III, it took over ten years to build the lavish Opéra Garnier. Construction was twice interrupted – by the Franco-Prussian War of 1870-1871 and again by the Paris Commune rebellion. The ceremonial official opening, featuring excerpts from Meyerbeer's *Les Huguenots* and Halévy's *La Juive*, took place in 1875. World-class operas and ballets were staged in the Opéra, one of the world's largest opera houses, until the opening of the Opéra Bastille in 1990. Today, it is exclusively ballet that is performed in the neo-baroque building, apart from the occasional operatic

# OPÉRA GARNIER 21

guest performances. It also houses a museum and a library devoted to the history of the opera. With the opening of the Opéra Bastille it was renamed Opéra Garnier in order to distinguish it from the new house – and ensure it now also pays homage to its architect, Charles Garnier.

The highlight of the Avenue de l'Opéra is the Palais Garnier (top). Everything here is magnificent – from the decorations of the balconies to the chandeliers. The impressive ceiling painting was created by Marc Chagall in 1963 (above).

# ÎLE DE LA CITÉ, RIVE DROITE

The Paris stock exchange has been in existence since 1724, initially at the Hôtel de Nevers. In 1808, Napoleon laid the foundation stone for the neo-classical Palais de la Bourse. It was designed by Alexandre Théodore Brongniart – and is therefore also known as Palais Brongniart. After Brongniart's death, Eloi Labarre took over the task of completing the building. In 1903 the palace was enlarged with two side wings, both perfectly matching the style of the main building. Trading on the floor began here in 1826. However, with the advent of computer trading in the 1990s, the stock

The exterior of the Stock Exchange is reminiscent of an ancient temple with Corinthian columns and a wide flight of steps. Inside it features a large hall (large picture) where once the floor trading took place, which could be observed from the surrounding gallery. Large letters in the frieze reveal the role of the temple-like structure: Bourse (top). The four statues in front of the stock exchange symbolize justice, trade, agriculture, and industry.

# PALAIS DE LA BOURSE

exchange lost its importance and so parts of the building are available today as a venue for various events, such as receptions, conferences, and seminars. The atmosphere in the Bourse is splendid, with a superb ceiling painting by Alexandre Abel de Pujo creating a stunning focal point.

# ÎLE DE LA CITÉ, RIVE DROITE

Cardinal Richelieu, Louis XIII's prime minister, commissioned the architect, Jacques Lemercier, to design Palais Royal, which was originally known as Palais Cardinal. After the death of Richelieu in 1642 the palace became the possession of the king, and has since been known as Palais Royal. Louis XIV spent part of his childhood in this stunning palace. A theater was built in one of the annexes, but it burned down. At the end of the 18th century it was rebuilt, and today is home to the famous Comédie Française. Beyond the palace, lie peaceful gardens, lined with stately arcaded buildings, put

# PALAIS ROYAL 23

up in the 1880s by Phillippe Egalite. Desperate to pay off his debts, he let out the some property as shops and flats which still remain. Famous intellectuals who lived in these homes include the writer, Colette, the author, painter, and director, Jean Cocteau, and the actor, Jean Marais.

In the past (top) as today, the Palais Royal gardens are ideal for a gentle stroll. They are also often used as a backdrop for filmmakers, for example for Stanley Donen in *Chara* with Audrey Hepburn and Cary Grant. The two fountains by Pol Bury (large picture) caused great controversy, and the black-and-white columns by Daniel Buren that were erected in the court yard in the 1980s proved to be even less popular.

Paris 61

# ÎLE DE LA CITÉ, RIVE DROITE

Les Halles was the traditional central market of Paris. In 1183, King Philippe II Auguste enlarged the marketplace in Paris and built a shelter for the merchants, who came to sell their wares. In the 1850s, the twelve halls of glass and iron buildings for which Les Halles became known, were constructed. Christened the "belly of Paris", in the famous book by Emile Zola, there was always a vibrancy about the market. However, in the 1960s the site became too small for the needs of the growing city and the market was moved to Rungis, south of Paris, despite vehement protests. The old

One of the main attractions for young visitors at the Forum des Halles is the old-fashioned merry-go-round (large picture). A typical feature of the shopping complex, which extends over four levels, some of which are underground, are the glass roofs supported by white arches. On the edges of the Forum stands Saint-Eustache, the Gothic church where Louis XIV, Madame de Pompadour, and Molière were christened (top).

62  Paris

# FORUM DES HALLES 24

halls meanwhile were demolished and the Forum des Halles built in its place. A huge mall, it comprises of more than 160 shops plus bank branches, post office, cinemas, restaurants and bars, an Olympic-sized swimming pool, the largest in Paris, as well as a merry-go-round for children.

# ÎLE DE LA CITÉ, RIVE DROITE

The Pompidou Centre, built by Renzo Piano and Richard Rogers, and opened in 1977, initially met with opposition – the building's flamboyant pipework which is exposed on the exterior, attracted unflattering nicknames such as "the fridge's backside". However, the Centre has now been one of the most visited city attractions for many years. It is home to the Musée National d'Art Moderne which regularly hosts every-changing special exhibitions, an arts complex and showcase for industrial design, a library, an arts cinema, the IRCAM (Institut de Recherche et Coordination Acoustique/

# CENTRE POMPIDOU 25

Musique), as well as an art bookshop, and cafés. A major attraction for visitors is the external escalator, which runs through transparent pipes providing views of Paris. The square in front of the complex is often bustling with visitors watching the street entertainers performing there.

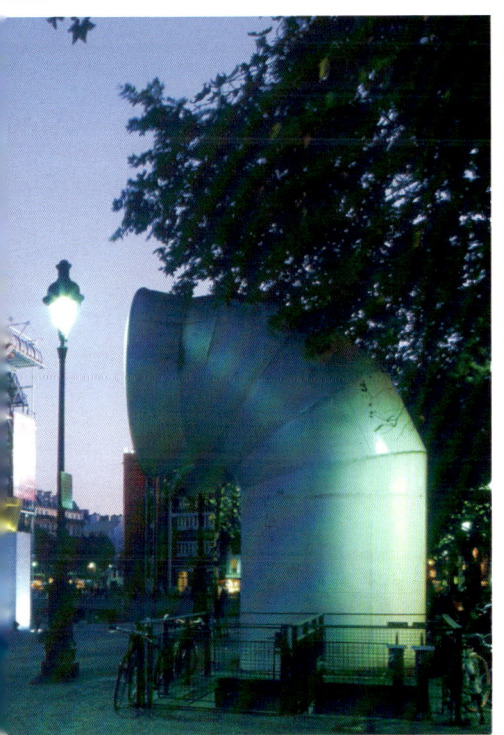

In front of the Centre Pompidou, the Stravinsky Fountau designed by Niki de Saint-Phalle and Jean Tinguely features bright sculptures spurting water (above). The Centre's façade and the escalators in plexiglass tubes, are now classic elements of modern architecture.

Paris 65

# ÎLE DE LA CITÉ, RIVE DROITE

The Hôtel de Ville, the seat of the city's government, is a late-19th-century building in the extravagant style of the neo-Renaissance and designed by the French architects, Théodore Ballu and Edouard Deperthes. The previous Hôtel de Ville also a Renaissance palace, was destroyed during the uprising of the Paris Commune in 1871. The façade of the present city hall features 146 statues of famous Parisian personalities, such as Eugène Delacroix, the historian and writer Jules Michelet, the actor François Joseph Talma, the sculptor Jean-Baptiste Pigalle, the creator of the gardens of Versailles,

# HÔTEL DE VILLE 26

André Le Nôtre, and Cardinal Richelieu. Since 1977 it has been the residence of the mayor of Paris – before that date, the city was governed by a prefect, just like all other French départements, and only the individual arrondissements or districts in Paris had their own mayor.

The façade of the city hall is embellished with an abundance of decorative elements and sculptures (above). The square in front of the building (large picture) has witnessed many gruesome scenes – for centuries, state executions were held here such as the murderer of King Henri IV, Ravaillac, who was quartered. Previously called Place de Grève, the square was renamed Place de l'Hôtel-de-Ville in 1803.

Paris 67

# ÎLE DE LA CITÉ, RIVE DROITE

The Marais (literally, the marsh) was drained by the Knights of the Templar in the 13th century and soon became the favoured area for the nobility and their magnificent city palaces. A number of these – the Hôtel de Sens, the Hôtel de Sully, and the Hôtel de Soubise – are preserved today. After the Revolution, the aristocrats moved away and artisans and small shop owners settled here instead. This piece of historic Paris was spared the urban transformations of Haussmann and was allowed to remain a district for local traders until almost the end of the 20th century.

About 600 years ago, the Marais was still outside the Paris city limits and the Jewish population was forced to settle here. Today, the main focus of Jewish life in Paris can still be found around the Rue des Rosiers with its busy kosher restaurants and shops (above).

# MARAIS

The Marais is now fashionable again with many chic shops. Also in the Marais is the Jewish quarter around the Rue des Rosiers, with kosher restaurants, shops and some of the oldest surviving houses in Paris. It is also home to the synagogue, designed by the architect, Hector Guimard.

## ÎLE DE LA CITÉ, RIVE DROITE

The oldest square in Paris, Place des Vosges, is bordered by arcaded pink brick and stone mansions with a garden in the middle. This masterpiece of architectural design was commissioned by King Henri IV as the Place Royale in 1605 and was inaugurated in 1612 for the wedding of Louis XIII to Anne of Austria. The façades of grey hewn stone and pale red brick as well as gray slate roofs with tall chimneys, create an enchanting picture. The square has been known by a number of different names during its history; its present one was given in 1800, as a tribute to the Département

# PLACE DES VOSGES

Vosges, which was the first area to pay its taxes. Many famous people have lived at the palace: Madame de Sévigné, the famous letter writer at the court of Louis XIV, was born here and the writers Victor Hugo, Théophile Gautier, and Alphonse Daudet all had homes in the famous Place.

The focal point of the Place des Vosges is its beautiful fountain, surrounded by immaculately maintained lawns and hedges (large picture). There are a number of restaurants underneath the mighty arcaded walkways of the city palaces (top), including the three-starred L'Ambroisie. Access to the square is via the gateways of the Pavillon du Roi in the south and the Pavillon de la Reine in the north (above).

Victor Hugo was born in 1802 in Besançon in eastern France – but he spent the major part of his life in Paris and died there in 1885. The poet and writer had a very turbulent early life. The son of an army general, he ventured far and wide as a child, growing up partly in Italy and in Spain. Throughout his life he was a highly politicized person, and he never shied away from denouncing abuses. After the coup d'état of Louis Napoléon Bonaparte, who crowned himself Emperor Napoleon III, Hugo had to flee the country. The first stop during his exile was Brussels, followed by the Channel island of Jersey, and from 1855 until his return to Paris in 1871, he lived on Guernsey. In his later years he was finally able to become politically active and was elected into the Senate in 1876. Victor Hugo is one of the most popular French poets and writers and only part of his

# VICTOR HUGO

prolific output is known in English – most famously *The Hunchback of Notre-Dame,* set against a backdrop of medieval Paris. Only experts know that aside from novels he also penned many poems and successful plays. His *Le roi s'amuse* was the model for Verdi's opera, *Rigoletto*.

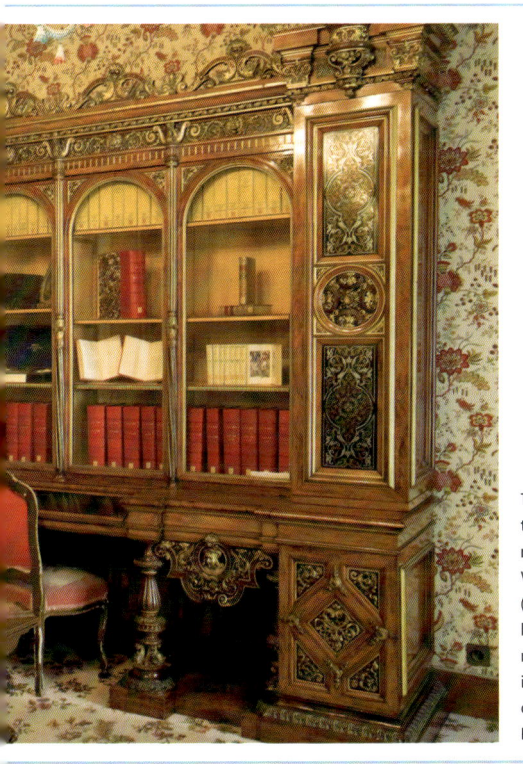

The fact that his apartment on the Place des Vosges is now a museum is proof of the respect Victor Hugo still commands (large picture). As well as Hugo's life and work, the museum also reflects the bourgeois lifestyle in the second half of the 19th century. The intellectual elite of Paris once met here (top).

French cuisine still enjoys an unrivalled reputation as one of the best in the world with many of the country's chefs gaining global recognition for their inspirational food and cooking techniques and their stylish restaurants. There are two institutions that assess and grade these restaurants: the food critics at Michelin award stars, while those from Gault-Millau award chef's hats. The freshness and combination of ingredients, and the chef's culinary skills is judged as is the degree of perfection in preparation and innovation. However, years of success do not guarantee awards. The Tour d'Argent, for a long time the flagship restaurant in Paris, lost two of its three stars in the past 15 years. In 2010, the Michelin guide awarded three stars to ten Parisian restaurants, two stars to 13 restaurants, and one star to 41 restaurants; these temples of excellent food are located

If you want to enjoy Frédéric Anton's cooking (top right) at the Pré Catelan you can combine this with a trip outside the city; the restaurant is located in the Bois de Boulogne. In a historical setting under the arcades of the Place des Vosges you'll find Bernard Pacaud's, L'Ambroisie (large picture). A truly delicious meal is always partnered with the perfect wine – and the sommeliers know which one to choose (above).

# MICHELIN-STARRED RESTAURANTS

throughout France, in both towns and citites. Chefs who hold awards can command top prices in their restaurants. However, if you are a lover of good food but don't wish to spend a fortune there's hope: many of these star chefs also run a second, less pricey restaurant or offer tasting menus.

# ÎLE DE LA CITÉ, RIVE DROITE

The storming of the Bastille prison in 1789, was the spark that ignited the beginning of the French Revolution. Now, nothing remains of the building. However, the square has preserved its symbolic importance, and each year on July 14, the French national holiday, Parisians still gather to commemorate the event. In the middle of the large square stands the Colonne de Juillet, the July Column, a reminder of the July Revolution in 1830. The figure on top of the column represents the spirit of liberty. The Opéra Bastille is one of the great projects initiated by the former President

# PLACE DE LA BASTILLE 29
# OPÉRA BASTILLE 30

François Mitterand. The Canadian architect Carlos Ott won the competition for its design. Its construction took longer than anticipated – the official inauguration was carried out on July 14 1989 ( the 200th anniversary of the Revolution) but regular performances did not start until March 1990.

The much-hated Bastille was destroyed down to its last stone in 1789-1790. Today, only Le Génie de la Liberté on top of the column in the middle of the square (large picture and above) recalls a revolution, albeit not the one of 1789, but the July revolution of 1830. Since 1989, another mighty structure has again dominated the square, the new Opéra Bastille (top), with an auditorium that accommodates 2,700 opera-goers.

Paris 77

The people's anger had been growing over many years. They bore the brunt of tax demands which were used to finance the royal family's expenditure, whereas the nobility and the clergy were exempt from taxation. The greatest discontent, however, was caused by the increase in the price of bread. Whether the Queen, Marie Antoinette, really said that if the people had no bread they should just eat cake, and whether this pronouncement really was the trigger for the Revolution can no longer be verified. Originally, the Bastille was a part of the city fortifications, serving as a prison from the 17th century. When the Bastille was stormed by the people of Paris however, on July 14, 1789, it held fewer than ten prisoners. But it was the symbol of the absolution of monarchy – and the French people were no longer willing to bow to the whims of the nobility. At first the king did not realize

# STORMING OF THE BASTILLE

what the consequences of the storming of the Bastille might be. The National Assembly sat at Versailles, and Louis XVI had been forced only recently to concede more rights to them. Only a few weeks later, on August 26, 1789, the Declaration of the Rights of Man and the Citizen was adopted.

The storming of the Bastille is impressively depicted in contemporary images. Jean-Baptiste Lallemand (top) and Jean-Pierre Houël (large picture) both show the battles that took place. Thanks to the National Assembly's adoption of Declaration of the Rights of Man and Citizen the French Revolution is still remembered.

Paris

Initially, French citizens did not want the monarchy abolished. A constitution was adopted to which Louis XVI agreed, opening the way for a constitutional monarchy. The mood changed with the flight of the royal family in June 1791 who were later caught in Varennes. The Revolution began with the storming of the Tuileries in August 1792. From March 1793 the revolutionary tribunal passed their judgment. Each day the carts full of those who were condemned to death were dragged to the guillotine on today's Place de la Concorde. Louis XVI was beheaded on January 21, and Marie Antoinette on October 16, 1793. The revolutionaries themselves also became the victims of the guillotine; as Girondist Pierre Vergniaud said when he ascended the scaffold: "The Revolution devours its own children". Georges Danton, an advocate and the first president of the Commit-

# THE FRENCH REVOLUTION

tee of Public Safety, and Camille Desmoulins, a journalist and a lawyer, were both executed on April 5 1794; Antoine de Saint-Just, a passionate follower of Robespierre, and Maximilien de Robespierre himself, a lawyer and leader of the Jacobins, died on the guillotine on July 28, 1794.

The best-known painting on the subject of the French Revolution, *Liberty leading the People* (large picture), was created by Eugène Delacroix in 1830. The execution of Louis XVI (top) is depicted here by an unknown artists whose painting hangs at the Musée Carnavalet. The revolutionary Jean-Paul Marat was stabbed in his bath by Charlotte Corday (above).

Paris 81

# ÎLE DE LA CITÉ, RIVE DROITE

The Musée Picasso owes its existence to a law passed by the French government in 1971, which allows heirs to pay some of their inheritance tax by ceding works of art to the state. Pablo Picasso had lived in France and kept a large number of his works in his own possession, and on his death, the French state acquired an extensive collection of his works including paintings, sculptures and pottery. They were at first exhibited in the Grand Palais and eventually found a permanent home in the Hôtel Salé in the Marais, which was converted for the purpose in 1985. The exhibition

The Hôtel Salé was commissioned by the tax collector Pierre Aubert and built around 1660. Its name – sale means salted – refers to the fact that Aubert was in charge of collecting the salt tax. The building with its grand staircase (top) had many different proprietors before being taken over by the city of Paris in 1962. After restoration, the works of Picasso found a permanent home here (large picture and above).

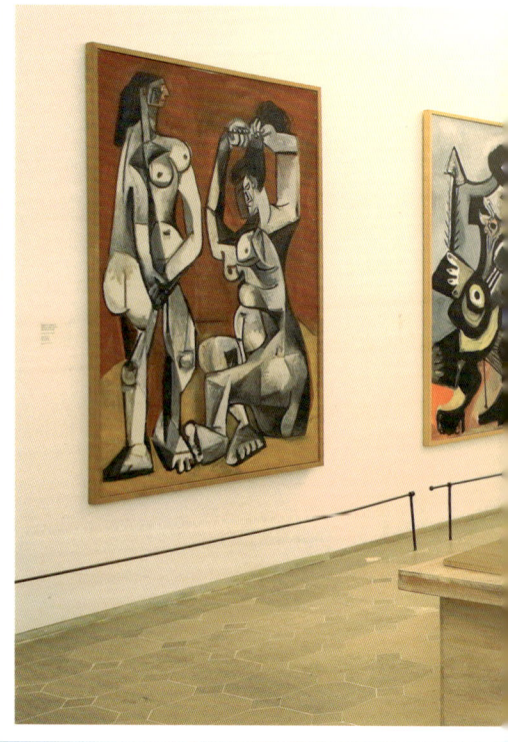

# MUSÉE NATIONAL PICASSO 31

starts with his Blue Period and his experiments with Cubism and moves on to large scale works on the theme of love, death, war and peace as well as portraits of his various muse. In the summer of 2009 the museum was closed for renovation work, which is due to be completed in 2012.

The Marais became part of Paris with the construction of a new city wall in the 14th century. The first palaces were built in the 16th century, but it was not until the start of the 17th century when King Henri IV had plans drawn up for the Place des Vosges – originally called Place Royale – that the district became fashionable among the nobility, who built magnificent palaces here. This popularity lasted until the 18th century. The Hôtel Carnavalet and the Hôtel de Soubise are two of the most splendid and well-maintained palaces. The former is the only remaining city palace from the 16th century – it was built for Jacques de Ligneris, who was president of the Law Court. In 1578, the palace passed into the ownership of Françoise de Kernevenoy, the widow of a Breton nobleman. Over time, the name became Carnavalet and the Carnavalet Museum (officially the Museum of the

# PALACES OF THE NOBILITY IN MARAIS

History of the City of Paris) has had its home here since the building was renovated in the late 19th century. In the 1730s, François de Rohan, Duke of Soubise, had the eponymous hôtel built and furnished in a splendid rococo style. Today the building houses part of the national archive.

Built in the 17th and 18th centuries for the nobility, many of the palaces of the Marais are open to the public. The Paris City Museum displays treasures in the Hôtel Carnavalet (large picture and above). Hôtel de Soubise (top) is home to part of the French national archive.

Paris 85

# ÎLE DE LA CITÉ, RIVE DROITE

If you've read *Foucault's Pendulum* by Umberto Eco, then you'll be aware of the Musée des Arts et Métiers, for this is where the most exciting action in the novel takes place – and where you can now see Foucault's original pendulum, which was used to definitively prove the rotation of the earth in 1851, and which once hung from the dome of the Panthéon in Paris. The museum, first established in 1802, was based on the collections of the Conservatoire National des Arts et Métiers (National Conservatory of Arts and Industry) one of the most important colleges in Paris. The exhibits are

# MUSÉE DES ARTS ET MÉTIERS

now on display in the magnificent rooms of the former abbey of the Saint-Martin-des Champs (church and monastic building), which was deconsecrated during the Revolution. The abbey now houses one of the world's most outstanding collections of scientific and industrial instruments.

As well as the exhibits, the rooms of the Musée des Arts et Métiers also deserve attention (large picture and top). The development of many mechanisms up to their industrial production is also explained (above). The Statue of Liberty shown in the museum was the first model created by Frédéric-Auguste Bartholdi.

The Panthéon at nightfall. The building's dome was designed at the end of the 8th century by Jacques-Germain Soufflot. In the background left, is the Tour Montparnasse, an office block built between 1969 and 1972.

# RIVE GAUCHE, QUARTIER LATIN

The Left Bank (Rive Gauche) is home to the narrow, winding streets and old buildings of the Quartier Latin (the Latin Quarter), which covers parts of the 5th and 6th arrondissements. The origins of the area's name stretch back to 1200 when all lessons at the Sorbonne, the oldest university in France, were held in Latin. Many bookshops opened up around this hub of knowledge and learning; but student life is not all hard work and studying, and a lively range of entertainment is available including restaurants serving food from around the world, cinemas, bars, and clubs – the Quartier is always bustling, both night and day.

# RIVE GAUCHE, QUARTIER LATIN

Saint-Germain-des-Prés is not just a district. The name stands for a whole way of life. During World War II and the postwar years, followers of the existentialist movement could be found in its cafés and restaurants, gathered around the famous existentialist writers, Jean-Paul Sartre and Simone de Beauvoir. The singer and actress, Juliette Gréco had her own bar, the "Tabou", where she appeared every evening, dressed entirely in black. For many years, Saint-Germain was also the district of bookshops and galleries; there are still many of these, but since Yves Saint-Laurent opened his

# SAINT-GERMAIN-DES-PRÉS

first prêt-à-porter shop "Rive Gauche" here in 1966, many other exclusive and expensive boutiques have arrived. The most influential publishing houses in France are based around the part-Romanesque, part early-Gothic church of Saint-Germain. The area is also popular for its late-night bars.

The streets of Saint-Germain-des-Prés (top) are full of life: the cafés and bistros, like the "Deux Magots" (left) are focal points for bohemians and intellectuals alike. Buildings of note include the Institut de France (above), meeting place of the Académie-Française and the church of Saint-Sulpice.

Paris 91

Dig deep into the history of the golden years of Saint-Germain-des-Prés and you will find that all roads lead to the writers, Simone de Beauvoir (1908–1986) and Jean-Paul Sartre (1905–1980). Sartre, above all, was the literary star around which the philosophical world of existentialism turned. Sartre and de Beauvoir met in 1929 and had a long, passionate but open relationship until Sartre's death. Both kept their own apartments all their lives. They frequently met at the famous cafés of Saint-Germain-des-Prés, such as the "Deux Magots" and the "Café de Flore", where they often worked on their current books. The literature of Simone de Beauvoir is strongly characterized by feminist thinking: *Memoirs of a Dutiful Daughter* or her famous roman-à-clef set in Saint-Germain, *The Mandarins*. Both Sartre and de Beauvoir deplored conformity and what they regarded as bourgeois lifestyle,

Simone de Beauvoir and Jean-Paul Sartre often shared their travels – to Rome (top), Brazil, and Moscow. During the 1968 May rebellion in Paris, they were supporters of the revolutionary students (large picture). The picture, above, shows Sartre as a soldier during World War II.

92 **Paris**

# JEAN-PAUL SARTRE AND SIMONE DE BEAUVOIR

strongly challenging their own upbringing. Sartre published many highly respected philosophical works (*Being and Nothingness*) as well as novels (*Nausea*) and dramas (*The Flies, No Exit*). He stood by his political, pro-Communist principles. In 1964, Satre refused the Nobel Prize for Literature.

The French chanson has a long tradition. Historians have even traced its roots back to François Villon, (1431 to circa 1463), the rebellious poet of the late Middle Ages, whose "*Ballade des Dames du Temps Jadis*" was reset to music in 1954 by Georges Brassens. Around the start of the 20th century, the mecca of the chanson was still Montmartre, with great names such as Mistinguett and Maurice Chevalier. In the 1930s and 1940s, stars such as Charles Trenet and Lucienne Boyer, were joined by singer/actors, Jean Gabin, Fernandel, and Arletty. In the post-war period, the many intimate venues of Saint-Germain-des-Prés and the Quartier Latin served as a springboard for several international careers. The songs of Edith Piaf, Juliette Gréco, Jacques Brel, Georges Brassens, Georges Moustaki, and Yves Montandare are still loved and respected today. The most important venue in

# CHANSONS

French light entertainment is not, however, on the Left Bank, but on the opposite side of the Seine on the Boulevard des Capucins, not far from the Opéra – the Olympia. A frail Edith Piaf appeared on stage here shortly before she died in 1963 at the tragically young age of 47.

Legendary chanson singers who have world-wide fame include the forever young Juliette Gréco (top); Charles Aznavour (left); the diminutive singer and actor; and Léo Ferré, whose songs often reflected his anarchic political views (above).

# RIVE GAUCHE, QUARTIER LATIN

The Sorbonne, founded in 1253 by the theologian Robert de Sorbon and confirmed by royal decree in 1257, is one of Europe's oldest universities and is still Paris's best known college. The present unified campus of buildings was designed in 1630 by the architect Jacques Lemercier on the orders of Cardinal Richelieu, its then President. The university's church is still one of the architectural highlights of Paris. Since its foundation, the Sorbonne has not only been a site for scholarly learning. It has also been a focal point for political unrest, most famously in May 1968 when student

# SORBONNE 34

protests led to street battles with police which sparked a general strike of about 10 million French workers. The action was also the trigger for protests at colleges in Europe and the US. As a consequence, the Sorbonne was divided into four separate universities to avoid further unrest.

The dome of the university church dominates the entire complex of buildings (top). Heated debate, an hour's rest between lectures or the romantic meeting place of young students in love – the cafés around the Place de la Sorbonne (left picture) are perfectly suited to life outside the lecture hall.

Paris 97

# RIVE GAUCHE, QUARTIER LATIN

The Panthéon looks back on a turbulent history. When he was seriously ill in 1744, Louis XIV vowed to build a church for Saint Genevieve, the patron saint of Paris, if he survived. On his recovery, he commissioned an architect Jacques-Germain Soufflot to draw up plans for the new church which was eventually completed in 1790. When the revolutionaries commissioned a deconsecration, declaring it a hall of glory, the building then became known as the Panthéon. Since 1885 many famous Frenchmen have found their final resting place here, often some years after their death. The first woman to

Below the Panthéon's dome, the physicist Jean Bernard Léon Foucault managed to bring proof of the Earth's rotation, using the pendulum that has since been named after him. The La Convention Nationale group of figures (large picture) was created by the sculptor François-Léon Sicard and installed in 1920. The French refer to the transfer of deceased dignitaries to the Panthéon as Panthéonization.

# PANTHÉON 35

be accorded a tomb was the prize-winning physicist Marie Curie in 1995. Other famous people buried in the Panthéon include the painter Jacques-Louis David, the writers Victor Hugo, Alexandre Dumas, Emile Zola and André Malraux, and the philosopher Voltaire and Jean-Jacques Rousseau.

Paris 99

In 486, Frankish troops under the leadership of the Merovingian king Clovis I inflicted a decisive defeat on the Romans at Soissons, north of Paris. In the years that followed, Clovis consolidated his power and converted to Christianity. It is not clear whether his baptism took place in 497, 498, or perhaps not until 507. However, by converting to Christianity King Clovis laid the foundations for creating his kingdom of the Franks, later to become France, one of the leading powers in mainland Europe. In 508, Clovis established Paris as the capital of his kingdom and the city was set on its path to becoming a world-ranking metropolis, although initially its significance declined. Clovis I divided his kingdom between his four sons; after his father's death in 511, Childebert I ruled over the area of the kingdom that included Paris. His brothers Theodoric, Clodomir and Clotaire had their own

Clovis I (top), the founder of the empire in which he united all the Franks, was of the utmost importance to the history of the city of Paris, especially because of his conversion to Christianity. A fresco in the Panthéon depicts him being baptized in the cathedral of Reims (top). A book illustration dating from the 15th century shows how Clovis divided up the empire among his sons (right).

100 Paris

# CLOVIS I

seats of government in Reims, Orléans and Soissons respectively. However, the balance of power changed when Charles the Great (Charlemagne) came to the throne as the Holy Roman Emperor. He moved his capital to the east to Aachen, leaving Paris only playing second fiddle in importance.

Paris 101

# RIVE GAUCHE, QUARTIER LATIN

The Palais du Luxembourg and the gardens that surround it were created in 1612 for Marie de' Medici, the widow of Henri IV. The 64-acre park is the green lung of the Quartier Latin and a meeting place for the local residents and the students at the Sorbonne and other nearby institutes. It is also a popular spot for tourists to relax. The park offers many leisure facilities for young and old. For the children, there are puppet performances, a playground with swings, and pony rides are often available; they can also sail boats on the large lake in front of the Palais building, a delightful pleasure the

The Palais du Luxembourg is the seat of the Senate, the second chamber of the French parliament (large picture). The baroque Jardin du Luxembourg offers a wonderfully tranquil setting for walkers as well as for those who just wish to simply enjoy the beautiful gardens (top); an artist captures the Fontaine de Médicis on canvas (above).

# JARDIN DU LUXEMBOURG

adults often indulge in, too. Adults can also play tennis or boules on gravel courts, compete at chess or enjoy concerts and opera performances in the Kiosque à Musique. Or visitors can simply indulge in a very Parisian activity: pause a little while, relax, and watch the world go by.

# RIVE GAUCHE, QUARTIER LATIN

The magnificent Palais at the heart of Jardin du Luxembourg tends to be ignored. This may be because the palace cannot be visited – it is the seat of the Senate, the second chamber of the French parliament. Maria de' Medici originally commissioned the Palais because, following the death of her husband, King Henry IV, she no longer wished to remain in her home at the Louvre. According to her vision, the Palais was to resemble the beautiful Palazzo Pitti in Florence, Italy. However the French architect, Salomon de Brosse was only marginally influenced by the Italian building and instead

# PALAIS DU LUXEMBOURG 37

designed a structure in the style of a French château. Up until the French Revolution in 1789, the building was occupied by Royalty; after that the Palais briefly became a prison with inmates such as Danton and Desmoulins, the famous revolutionaries. Since 1852 the Senate has had its seat here.

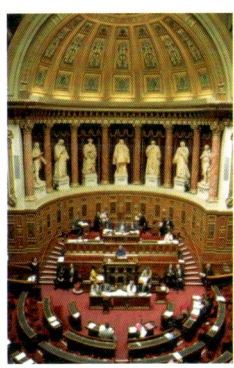

The Palais du Luxembourg rises majestically above the great lake where small boats sail (top). Only a few of the parliamentarians will appreciate their magnificent surroundings, such as for the glorious assembly hall (above). The grand staircase (large picture) makes an attractive backdrop for many a political group photograph.

# RIVE GAUCHE, QUARTIER LATIN

Imposing, futuristic, but also with a distinct air of the Orient and the exotic, Jean Nouvel and a group of French architects designed this modern building for the Institut du Monde Arabe (Arab World Institute) in the 1980s, taking their inspiration from classical Arabian design. The windows, which are in the moucharaby style, have screens of intricate latticework traditionally used to protect interiors from the sun and people from the gaze of those outside. The windows also react to the light, opening and closing like the apperture of a traditional camera lens. The institute's mission is to

Decorated with mosaics, wood-carving, and wrought iron, the Mosquée de Paris displays fine Moorish ornamentation (above). Non-Muslim guests can relax in the Turkish baths or hannan (large picture). Architect Jean Nouvel is responsible for the striking design of the Institut du Monde Arabe (top).

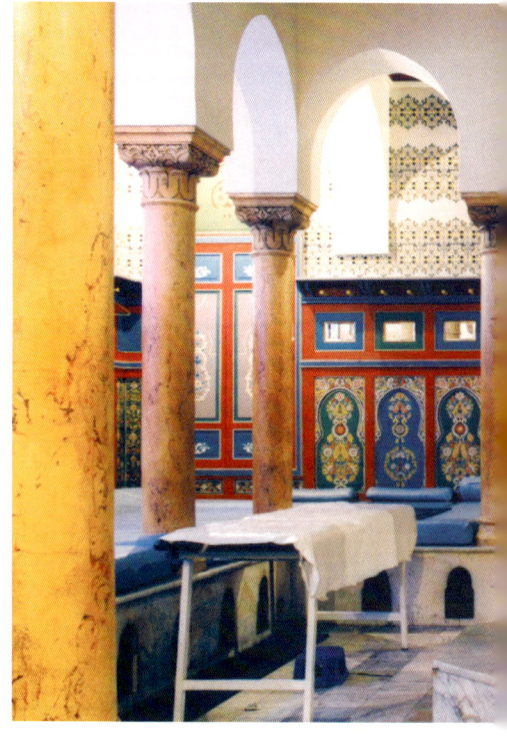

# INSTITUT DU MONDE ARABE
# THE PARIS MOSQUE

promote cultural exchange and to encourage relations between the Arab world, France and Europe through events and exhibitions. The Paris Mosque was built between 1922 and 1926 and is open to non-Muslims. You can enjoy a Turkish hamam bath experience, and sample pastries and mint tea.

# RIVE GAUCHE, QUARTIER LATIN

When the Gare d'Orsay was opened as the terminus of the Paris-Orléans Railway for the World Exhibition in 1900, it was one of the most modern railway stations in France. However, by the end of the 1930s the building was no longer able to meet the demands of technical developments in rail transport, and was closed. In 1978 the station was listed as an historic building and in 1980 work began converting it into a museum. From 1982, the project was supervised by the architect, Gae Aulenti, from Milan who made creative use of the beautiful glass roof over the former concourse to create

The complete transformation of the station by the Milanese architect Gae Aulenti in 1982 provides the perfect backdrop for the works of art displayed in the Musée d'Orsay (large picture and above). It is mainly from the outside that the former use of the structure on the banks of the Seine becomes apparent (top).

108 Paris

# MUSÉE D'ORSAY 40

a bright, central hall flooded with natural light. Today, the museum displays masterpieces of French art, with an emphasis mainly on the second half of the 19th century. Its comprehensive collection of Impressionist works include treasures by Degas, Manet, Monet, Renoir, and Pissarro.

The Musée d'Orsay has one of the most important collections of Impressionist works in the art world today. The painting that gave the movement its name Claude Monet's *Impression, Soleil Levant* (*Impression, Sunrise*) hangs in the Musée Marmottan in Paris (2 rue Louis-Boilly, Métro Muette).

The Impressionists abandoned their studios to paint from nature, intent on depicting the moods created by different qualities of light. This was shown in Claude Monet's series of paintings in which Rouen Cathedral is always depicted from the same angle but at a different time of the day and in different weather conditions. The paint was often applied in a short, stippled fashion, without clear outlines so that different hues combined to create a new shade. The Impressionist artists also abandoned traditional topics; they chose landscapes and scenes of day-to-day life over religion,

# IMPRESSIONISTS

or history. Artists of the movement include Claude Monet, Edouard Manet, Edgar Degas, Auguste Renoir, Alfred Sisley, Camille Pissarro, and the American Mary Cassatt. Claude Debussy was perhaps the foremost "musical impressionist", along with Maurice Ravel and Paul Dukas.

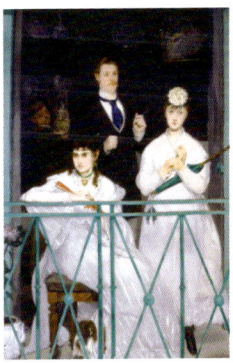

The Musée d'Orsay has achieved renown with its fantastic Impressionist collection. World-famous paintings are exhibited here such as Claude Monet's *The Poppy Field,* (1873) (top). Large pictures from the left: Edgar Degas' *The Dance Class* (1874) and Auguste Renoir's *Dance in the City* (1883). Above: Edouard Manet's *The Balcony* (1868).

Paris 111

Three artists widely represented in the Musée d'Orsay were responsible for laying the foundations of modern styles such as Expressionism and Cubism. Paul Gauguin, the only Parisian of the three, did not produce his main paintings in Paris, but initially worked in Brittany, particuarly in Pont-Aven, and from 1891 on the Polynesia islands. Many of his paintings were idealized representations of the lives of the Polynesians. The Dutchman Vincent van Gogh gained most of his stimulus for painting in Paris, but only found his true style in Arles in Provence. Van Gogh was inspired by the distinctive quality of the light in the landscape there. In an amazing burst of creativity he produced more than 180 paintings in just 16 months. He then returned to Auvers-sur-Oise in the Île-de-France region, where he ended his life in 1890. Born in Aix-en-Provence, Paul Cézanne was never completely at home in

# PIONEERS OF MODERN ART

Paris and after a few years returned to Provence where he produced his principal works. His style is characterized by repetitive, small brushstrokes. However different these three artists are in style, their striking use of glowing hues, applied with forceful brushstrokes, unite them in common ground.

Evolution in form, hue and expression: Paul Cézanne was an Impressionist, but later found his own, new style, as demonstrated in his painting *Vessels, Basket, and Fruit* (top). Other pioneers of modern art: Vincent van Gogh and his *Bedroom at Arles* (large picture); and Paul Gauguin's *The Meal and Tahitian Women* (*On the Beach*) (small pictures above).

Paris 113

# RIVE GAUCHE, QUARTIER LATIN

An evening stroll along the banks of the Seine is one of the most romantic forms of relaxation the French capital offers. Without the Seine, Paris would simply not be Paris. The third longest river in France at 482 miles (775 km), the Seine rises in Burgundy and flows into the English Channel at Le Havre. The banks of the Seine in the heart of the city were declared a UNESCO World Heritage Site in 1991. The ship that features on Paris' coat of arms signifies the importance of the river as a vital transport route. The heraldic motto, Fluctuat, nec mergitur, translates as: "She is tossed upon the waves but

# RIVER SEINE 41

not overwhelmed". Luckily, the plans of the former president Georges Pompidou, to build expressways along the river banks, never came to fruition. And in the summer, a long stretch of the right bank is lined with sand, complete with deck chairs, parasols, and palm trees – "Paris-on-Sea".

The Île de la Cité with its gothic cathedral, Notre-Dame, rests in the middle of the river like a giant ship. You can get great views of the church's apse from the Quai d'Orléans on the Ile Saint-Louis (large picture) and can climb one of the towers in Notre-Dame and vew the Seine from up high (above). House boats are moored along the Seine banks; top: with the Alexandre III bridge in the background.

Paris 115

If you enjoy wandering around markets, there are plenty of opportunities in the heart of the French capital. Each arrondissement holds different types of markets on various days of the week. The largest flower market in Paris is located on the Île de la Cité, only a stone's throw from Notre-Dame. On Sundays – aside from a sea of flowers – the most diverse species of birds are also available. Food markets thrive in most arrondissements and the market on the Rue Mouffetard in the Quartier Latin, in particular, is a great insight into French culinary life. The Marché Biologique, the organic market on Boulevard Raspail (Métro Notre-Dame-des-Champs), is held on Sundays. For something a little different try the market located under the Barbès-Rochechouart metro station (where the metro becomes an elevated railway). It caters for the high proportion of African and Arab residents in the sur-

# MARKETS

rounding district of Goutte d'Or. But the most popular market for tourists, at least those interested in antiques, lies on the outskirts of Paris – the "Marché aux Puces", the Saint-Ouen flea market which is open on Saturday, Sunday and Monday. Nearest metro is Porte de St-Ouen.

There are numerous markets in Paris's various districts, offering a great variety of fresh foods for sale. One of the best-known, with a long tradition, is based in the Rue Mouffetard in the Quartier Latin (top). The most famous fleamarket (marché aux puces) in the world is found in Saint-Ouen to the north of Paris (above and large picture).

Paris 117

From the Eiffel Tower you can enjoy fabulous views across the Parc du Champs and the Parc de Mars to the École Militaire (large picture).

# FAUBOURG SAINT-GERMAIN

Unlike the lively, bustling Latin Quarter with its artists and students and their 24-hour lifestyle, the Faubourg Saint-Germain is a particularly quiet district where many ministries and embassies are located – the French prime minister's residence is here. This former residential suburb is also home to several major Parisian attractions, such as the Eiffel Tower, the Musée Rodin, the Hôtel, and Dôme des Invalides, and, just a short trip across the Seine, the Palais de Chaillot and the Palais de Tokyo with its contemporary art museums. There are also many antique shops and art galleries in the eastern part of the district.

# FAUBOURG SAINT-GERMAIN

The original Palais Bourbon structure, the core of which has mostly been retained, was built between 1722 and 1728 for Louise Françoise de Bourbon, the daughter of King Louis XIV. In 1765, her grandson and heir, the Prince de Condé, had the Palais extended using a design by Jacques-Germain Soufflot. Under state control during the French Revolution, a classical portico was later added on its Seine side that mirrored the Madeleine Church at the other end of the axis between Place de la Concorde and the Rue Royale. The Palais has been a political meeting place since 1827, first for the lower House

# PALAIS BOURBON 42

of Parliament and then, from 1849, for the French National Assembly. Additional work was carried out to meet the requirements of the government; the painter Eugène Delacroix, later elected a representative himself, was one of those who worked on the interior design of the Palais Bourbon.

The French parliament, the National Assembly, meets at the Palais Bourbon. Among its lavishly furnished rooms is a magnificent library (large picture).

Paris 121

# FAUBOURG SAINT-GERMAIN

The Musée Rodin is located in the Hôtel Biron, a large palace built in the rococo style by Jean Aubert in 1729–1730 and bears the name of one of its previous owners, the Maréchal de Biron. The great sculptor and painter Auguste Rodin rented rooms here in 1908 at the suggestion of his secretary, the German poet Rainer Maria Rilke, since the spacious building already contained an artist's studio. In 1911, the state took over the building and the residents had to move out, but Rodin was reluctant to leave the quartier. However, the government granted him the right to live in the building

# MUSÉE RODIN 43

for the rest of his life in return for his estate. A pioneer of modern art, Rodin died in 1917 and the museum was opened in 1919. In addition to his works, Rodin's own art collection is exhibited as well as works by his student and one-time lover, Camille Claudel, sister of the poet Paul Claudel.

The Musée Rodin (top) has an extensive collection of the great artist's work. Sculptures such as *The Kiss* (above) and, in the large image, the study for his famous statue, *The Burghers of Calais*, show that Rodin's unique style looked forward towards the modern age.

Paris 123

# FAUBOURG SAINT-GERMAIN

Louis XIV built the Hôtel des Invalides for soldiers who were wounded in the campaigns fought during his reign (1643–1715). The name is derived from its original function as a hospital. A highlight of the building complex, designed by Libéral Bruant and completed in 1676, is the church constructed in the last decades of the 17th century to designs by Jules Hardouin-Mansart. Its impressive cupola was freshly gilded in 1989 for the bicentennial anniversary of the Revolution. Directly below the cupola is the red marble sarcophagus of Emperor Napoleon I, which conceals five further

The dome of Les Invalides reaches to the sky on the Left Bank of the Seine (large picture). The fresco in the cupola is by Charles de la Fosse (top). Playful putto provide charming decorations (above).

124 Paris

# HÔTEL AND DÔME DES INVALIDES

coffins made from tinplate, mahogany, lead, ebony, and oak. The Hôtel des Invalides is also home to several specialist museums well worth visiting: the Musée de l'Armée, the Musée de l'Ordre de la Libération, the Musée d'Histoire Contemporaine, and the Musée des Planset des Reliefs.

"History is a lie on which everyone is agreed", Napoleon is believed to have said. Born on August 15, 1769 in Corsica, Napoleon Bonaparte graduated from the French military school and was appointed an artillery officer in the army in 1785. In 1799, he declared himself a First Consul, and five years later, the French proclaimed him Emperor. In the first decade of the 19th century, the French Empire under Napoleon engaged in a series of conflicts, the Napoleonic Wars, involving every major European power. After a series of victories, the French invasion of Russia in 1812 marked a turning point in Napoleon's fortunes. His army was badly defeated in this campaign and he never fully recovered. In 1813, the Sixth Coalition defeated his forces at Leipzig; the following year the Coalition invaded France and forced Napoleon to abdicate. He was then exiled to the island of Elba. Less than a

# NAPOLEON BONAPARTE

year later, he escaped Elba and returned to power, but was beaten by Nelson's troops at the Battle of Waterloo in June 1815. Napoleon spent the last six years of his life under British supervision on the island of St Helena, off the Italian coast, where he died on May 5, 1821 from cancer.

Napoleon's remains are kept at the Dôme des Invalides in a total of five stacked sarcophagi, the outer one made from a reddish brown quartzite (large picture). Jacques-Louis David, the famous painter closely linked with the Revolution, depicted the coronation ceremony for Napoleon and Joséphine in 1804 (top). One of the numerous portraits of the Corsican, by Paul Delaroche (above).

Paris 127

# FAUBOURG SAINT-GERMAIN

When the first funeral took place in the Montparnasse cemetery in 1824, it was still located beyond the confines of the city. Today it offers an oasis of peace in the very lively Montparnasse district in the 14th arrondissement. At just under 50 acres (20 hectares) this is not just one of Paris' largest cemeteries, but also a park with more than 1,200 trees. Over the years, countless celebrities from different countries have found their final resting place here, including the Irish playwright Samuel Beckett, the Romanian writer Eugène Ionesco, the American actress Jean Seberg, as well as

# MONTPARNASSE CEMETERY 45

many famous French people such as Charles Garnier who built the Opéra, the singer Serge Gainsbourg, film director, Eric Rohmer and the gastronomer, Pierre Larousse. You can also see the works of some famous sculptors; Rodin, Jean Arp, and Niki de Saint-Phalle are all represented.

Many of the graves have particularly gruesome reminders of death and the tombs often reveal tales from the past (large picture). The author, Simone de Beauvoir and her partner, the writer and philosopher Jean-Paul Sartre, rest in Montparnasse (above).

No one knows exactly how many bistros (also spelled bistrots) there are in Paris. Nor does anyone really know the true origin of the name. It is said that when the Russian soldiers who occupied Paris during the Napoleonic wars demanded faster service in the hotels they shouted "bistro" (quickly) in Russian. Another theory is that the term came from the colloquial French word, bistouille, meaning a mix of brandy and coffee. Whatever the history of the word, one thing is certain: the bistro is as popular as it ever was and can be found in the elegant western districts of Paris as well as in the less affluent eastern areas. Most bistros today offer their customers a printed menu, not – as was customary – a slate black board where the day's specials were chalked up every morning. Many bistros no longer charge less for the coffee or the red wine if it is consumed at the bar – au

# LE BISTRO

zinc – as was once the order of the day. However, this does not stop the French from dropping into their local bistro at all times of the day – in the early morning for breakfast, at lunchtime for the menu du jour, and in the evening for a meal or a glass of wine and the latest gossip with the locals.

Most bistros have pavement tables and chairs – in winter heaters are installed – because the Parisians love to see and be seen whether they're in Saint-Germain-des-Prés (above) or the Champs-Elysées (large picture). The bistro is always a great place to meet up for a speedy espresso, glass of wine or a five-course meal.

# FAUBOURG SAINT-GERMAIN

The Eiffel Tower, the symbol of Paris and the city's tallest building, was constructed for the World Exhibition and centenary of the Revolution in 1889. Originally planned to last just 20 years, its construction led to protests by prominent figures, including writers Guy de Maupassant, the architect, Alexandre Dumas, Charles Garnier, and composer Charles Gounod. With time, Parisians accepted the Tower, and thanks to its radio mast it also fulfilled a practical function. Including its mast, the Eiffel Tower rises to over 300 yd (324 m). Ten thousand tonnes of puddled iron (a type

# EIFFEL TOWER 46

of wrought iron) were used in its construction, and the Tower requires a fresh coat of paint every four years. Lifts rise to the three platforms, but energetic visitors can take the stairs to the first and second platforms where there are souvenir shops, a restaurant, and snack bar.

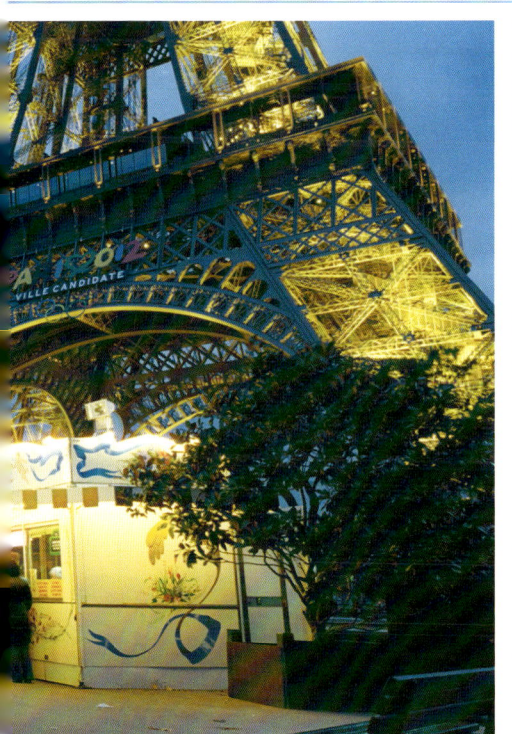

Wherever it's viewed from, such as the Champ-de-Mars (large picture), the Eiffel Tower is impressive. When illuminated at night, its famous iron skeleton is a magical sight and long beams from its powerful searchlights penetrate the night sky.

Paris 133

The best-known structure in Paris, the Eiffel Tower, was created not by an architect but by an engineer. Born in Dijon in 1832, Gustave Eiffel's ancestors had come to France from the Eifel region in Germany. Gustave studied at the École centrale des arts et manufactures in Paris and received his degree in chemical engineering in 1855. The young engineer reached a turning point in his career when Charles Nepveu, owner of a steel company, employed him in the railway bridge construction department. The first major project Eiffel managed was the great rail bridge in Bordeaux, and he went on to supervise other projects not only in France but also across Europe (Hungary, Romania, Portugal, Switzerland) and in South America. As well as the Eiffel Tower, he was also responsible for the interior wrought-iron structure that supports the Statue of Liberty in New York. But he will remain

# GUSTAVE EIFFEL

inextricably linked with the iconic tower that bears his name, which proved that when intelligently combined, technology and functionality can create a beauty of their own. The engineer had strong emotional links with "his" tower – he even had his own apartment at the top.

The master photographed in 1890 and his work. His contemporaries closely monitored the construction of the tower, many with great suspicion. Revolutionary for its day, a special metal, puddle iron, was used that could be elegantly worked as seen in the detailed photographs.

# FAUBOURG SAINT-GERMAIN

The Musée du Quai Branly – or the Musée des Arts et Civilisations d'Afrique, d'Asie, d'Océanie, et des Amériques – is housed in an innovative glass building set on stilts. This ultra-modern museum of ethnology was designed by Jean Nouvel and has drawn crowds of visitors since its opening in 2006. Its 300,000 exhibits give a fascinating insight into the cultures of the wide range of ethnic groups who populate the geographical regions of Africa, Asia, Oceania, and the Americas. The collection was designed with education in mind and provides information on many civilizations, ancient

The museum at the Quai Branly was created in the early 21st century for all those interested in the diversity of the world's population (large picture). The collections have been newly designed and laid out according to the latest educational thinking, and introduce visitors into the world of ethnic groups in Africa, the Americas, Asia, Australia, and Oceania (above and top right).

# MUSÉE DU QUAI BRANLY 47

and modern, by focusing on art, religion, culture, and customs in an accessible way, for both adults and children. The museum is set in a large garden and this "nature" theme is further emphasized by a huge "living wall", a long exterior wall on which thousands of plants and ferns grow.

# FAUBOURG SAINT-GERMAIN

In common with the nearby Palais de Chaillot, the stunning art deco Palais de Tokyo was constructed for the World Exhibition in 1937. Since 1961, it has been the home of the Musée d'Art Moderne de la Ville de Paris, a collection that includes important works such as *La Danse* by Matisse and the enormous *La Fée Electricité* by Raoul Dufy. Paris has a reputation for embracing the new, and modern art is well represented in the city. The Site de Création Contemporaine at the Palais de Tokyo, established in 2002, houses temporary exhibitions in all areas of cutting-edge contemporary art

Both 20th-century and contemporary works of art can be found in the Palais de Tokyo (top). Once you've admired the paintings such as this work by Matthew Ritchie (large image) the museum's stylish restaurant (above) is an inviting place in which to rest and recharge your batteries with coffee and cake.

138 Paris

# PALAIS DE TOKYO

(painting, sculpture, graphic art, photography, video, design, installations, fashion, and dance). And art is not just restricted to the exhibition area – the restaurant floor is decorated with a work featuring floral motifs by the artist Michael Lin, which also carries over to the walls.

# FAUBOURG SAINT-GERMAIN

The Île des Cygnes (Island of Swans) takes its name from the earlier island that was once attached to the bank of the Seine at the Champ-de-Mars in the late 18th century. Today's Île des Cygnes is an artificially created island 973 yards (890 m) long and just 22 yards (20 m) wide. A tree-lined path runs its length, providing a pleasant walk and a view of the Maison de l'ORTF, housing the French public service radio broadcaster, on the opposite bank. The island's main claim to fame is the small replica of New York's Statue of Liberty located at the southern end. The island's Liberty is just one quarter the

# LIBERTY STATUE 49
# ÎLE DES CYGNES 50

size of her big sister, who was sculpted by Auguste Bartholdi and presented to the United States by France in 1886. She looks west towards America, the book in her hand bearing the inscription "IV Juillet 1776 = XIV Juillet 1789", the dates of the American and French Revolutions.

You may think you've arrived in New York, when you see the Statue of Liberty (above). But the Paris replica of Lady Liberty measures 11.5 m (37ft 7in) in height. The Pont de Bir-Hakeim (top) is one of the capital's most attractive bridges. In the large picture the northern end of the Île des Cygnes can be seen, complete with the equestrian statue known as *La France renaissante*.

Paris 141

The Grande Arche, completed for the bicentenary of the French Revolution in 1989, forms one end point of the "axe historique". The arch in the La Défense district of skyscrapers houses offices and a ministery.

# FURTHER AFIELD

The inner city of Paris is a wealth of architectural masterpieces, museums, galleries and beautifuly designed parks. But it is well worth taking the time to venture a little further and explore the outer edges of the city. You enter an entirely different world here – the buzzing and lively streets and alleyways of Montmartre around Sacré-Coeur, the elegance and tranquillity in the parks and the rural and idyllic Bois de Boulogne. If, however, inspiring modern technology or classical music is more your style, you'll feel at home among the highrise buildings of La Défense and in the spectacular Parc de la Villette complex.

## FURTHER AFIELD

The Bois de Boulogne has something for everyone – a large English-style park with picturesque lakes and waterfalls, and the small Bagatelle chateau and gardens and was created as the result of a wager. The Count of Artois, brother of Louis XVI, bet Marie Antoinette that he could construct a chateau and garden in record time. Two months later La Bagatelle was complete. The park also includes the Jardin de Shakespeare with an open-air stage, the Jardin d'Acclimatation, a childrens' amusement park with a zoo, the Serres d'Auteuil (19th-century glass houses and gardens), the

A highlight of the Bois de Boulogne is the small chateau of La Bagatelle and its gardens (large picture and top), with a number if enchanting pavilions (above). You can also take a stroll along the banks of the peaceful lake.

# BOIS DE BOULOGNE 51

Musée des Arts et Traditions (folklore museum), the Pré Catelan and Grande Cascade restaurants, the Auteuil and Longchamp racecourses, the Parc des Princes stadium, home of football team Paris Saint-Germain, and the Roland Garros tennis courts, where the French open is played.

**Paris** 145

Paris has six major terminal stations. Trains arrive at the Gare du Nord Trains from England on Eurostar, the north of France, Belgium and west Germany; trains from the Alsace, the rest of Germany and Eastern Europe terminate at the Gare de l'Est; the Gare de Lyon is the terminus for trains from southern France and Italy; the Gare d'Austerlitz from the Loire valley and the Dordogne; the Gare Montparnasse from western and southwest France; and finally the Gare Saint-Lazare where trains from Normandy arrive. All the station were built between the middle of the 19th and the beginning of the 20th century. The magnificent structures have still largely kept their original appearance. The Gare de Lyon has a fabulous restaurant, Le Train Bleu, named after the famous French luxury night express service, which carried wealthy European passengers to the French Riviera, to escape

# THE STATIONS OF PARIS

the winter. Its superbly furnished room featues paintings which depict scenes from the south of France. The Gare d'Orsay, like the Gare de Lyon, built for the World Exhibition in 1900, was converted in the 1980s to one of the city's most popular museums, showing the work of the Impressionists.

With their magnificent architecture and lavish sculptural ornamentation, the Paris stations are witness to a time when rail travel was still reserved for the privileged few. At the Gare du Nord (all pictures), for example, past and present coincide today when a modern train, such as the high-speed TGV (large picture bottom) arrives on one of the platforms.

# FURTHER AFIELD

Plans for the great commercial district to the west of Paris began in the mid-1950s. The first building, the CNIT (Centre de Nouvelles Industries et Technologies), opened in 1958 and remains an architectural highlight. The first high-rise buildings appeared in the 1970s, provoking a major storm of protest as they altered the view from the Champs-Élysées to the west. Later – particularly in the 1980s – the tower blocks multiplied and grew skyward, and today many large French companies have their headquarters here. The architectural jewel in the crown, the Grande Arche, was

# LA DÉFENSE 52

inaugurated in 1989. This completed the "axe historique", an historical line of vision running through the western part of the city, from the Arc de Triomphe du Carrousel by the Louvre, through the Arc de Triomphe to the Grande Arche on Place Charles de Gaulle at the top of the Champs-Élysées.

Glass and steel are the predominant materials used in the sky scraper district of La Défense. The mighty Grande Arche (top), designed by Danish architect Jens Otto von Spreckelsen, is a major focal point, with a height of 110 m (360 ft). In many places, sculptures relax the chilly atmosphere of the office tower blocks, as for example the "Tête monumentale" (giant head) by the Polish sculptor Igor Mitoraj (large picture).

Paris 149

# FURTHER AFIELD

The years 1870 and 1871 were marked by traumatic events for France, and Paris in particular, with defeat in the Franco-Prussian War and the loss of Alsace-Lorraine, as well as the suppression of the uprising of the revolutionary Paris Commune. The Sacré-Coeur was built between 1876 and 1914 as a symbol of atonement, but also of strength and new beginnings. Although the architect, Paul Abadie, drew on many styles, he primarily used the Byzantine-inspired cathedral of Périgueux as a model for the white stone building that is now one of the most-visited monuments of Paris.

# SACRÉ-COEUR 53

If the prospect of climbing the 200 or so steps up to Sacré-Coeur from the bottom of the hill is too much, take the funicular railway. The dome gallery offers an unmatched view over Paris. A visit to the adjacent church of Saint-Pierre, one of the oldest buildings in Paris, is worthwhile.

Two structures dominate the skyline of Paris: the Eiffel Tower and the magnificent Sacré-Coeur (large picture and above). Built on the butte (hill), the cathedral, with its gleaming white domes and bell tower is the highest point in the city. The area around the Sacré-Coeur is the heart of Montmartre with picturesque alleys and restaurants (top).

Paris 151

# FURTHER AFIELD

According to legend, the name of Montmartre comes from the Latin mons martyrum (martyr's hill), as this is where St Dionysius, the first Bishop of Paris, was beheaded. However, it may derive from mons martis (hill of Mars) after a shrine to the Roman god Mars that was located here. The area became a haven for artists during the belle époque, their permissive lifestyle scandalizing the more conventional local residents. Cabaret venues such as at the Moulin Rouge were established, whose risqué cancan shows even managed to lure in some of the city's more "respectable" citizens. The

Time stands still in the narrow streets of Montmartre (large picture and top). Right in the heart of Montmartre, on the Place du Tertre, you'll find cabaret shows, such as the La Crémaillère 1900 (above), which is also a restaurant.

152 **Paris**

# MONTMARTRE 54

Moulin Rouge still attracts the crowds while visitors also flock to the cafés and restaurants around the Place du Tertre, the heart of Montmartre. Relax with a glass of wine and soak up the atmosphere created by today's artists although you're unlikely to find a budding Lautrec among them.

Paris at night conjures up images of the Moulin Rouge, the Lido, the Crazy Horse, and Toulouse-Lautrec's sketches of high-kicking, "Doriss Girls", cancan dancers. The Moulin Rouge in Montmartre, has been situated on the Place Blanche since 1889, the Lido on the Champs-Élysées since 1946, and the Crazy Horse in the elegant Avenue George V, near the Champs-Élysées, since 1951. At these venues the dinner shows are glitzy and kitsch and predominantly feature the skimpily dressed dancers. However, young people looking for a different type of entertainment are spoilt for choices. For some years now there has been a lively clubbing and disco scene in the Bastille area and especially around Rue Oberkampt, offering both top DJs and live music. In the clubs around the Champs Élysées the rich and beautiful hit the dancefloor. And if you're not interested in

# PARIS NIGHTLIFE

Parisian bars and clubs, you may wish to watch a production of one of France's classic dramatists such as Racine which are enjoyable, even if your French is basic. Or you can listen to one of the famous French chansonniers in concert at the legendary Olympia on the Boulevard des Capucines.

The Moulin Rouge cabaret (top) is located in Montmartre, historically the entertainment district of Paris. When top DJs appear at the trendy clubs around the Rue Oberkampf and on the Champs-Élysées, young people hit the dancefloor (above). Before visiting the district's clubs, you can eat at the restaurants in the Quartier Latin, which serve food from the varied cuisines around the world (large picture).

His posters offer instant time-travel back to the belle époque, giving a "warts and all" view of the nightlife around Montmartre at that time. The painter and graphic artist Henri de Toulouse-Lautrec, was born in 1864 in Albi, in the south of France, into one of the oldest French aristocratic families, the counts of Toulouse. Suffering from an inherited disease, his growth was stunted and he only reached a height of 1.52 m (4 ft 11 in). He decided to become a painter when he was still at school and in 1882 he arrived in Paris to study the academic style of painting of that time. However, he soon developed his own genre. The glittering world of Montmartre was a powerful attraction for him, and in 1884 he moved to an apartment close to the Place Blanche, where a few years later the Moulin Rouge opened its doors. This exotic environment shaped both the painter and

# HENRI DE TOULOUSE-LAUTREC

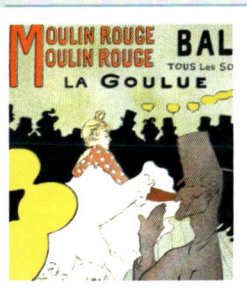

his work. He designed posters for cabarets such as the Moulin Rouge and the singer and comedian, Aristide Bruant, commissioned posters for his cabaret, Le Mirliton. Lautrec was a notorious alcoholic with a taste for absinthe. That and syphilis eventually led to his death in September, 1901.

Toulouse-Lautrec was famed for the posters he created for the cabarets of Montmartre which showcased artistes such as the dancer Jane Avril (above and top right), the chansonnier Aristide Bruant (large picture) and La Goulue (top left).

# FURTHER AFIELD

A stroll along the Canal Saint-Martin introduces visitors to a different Paris, far removed from the historic buildings, galleries, and iconic monuments. In the streets around the canal you can still find artisans and traders enjoying a coffee or an aperitif in a local bar, carrying out their daily shopping, and generally going about their business. Fans of French cinema may recognize the Canal Saint-Martin — even if it was recreated in the studio — as it was used as the backdrop for the 1938 classic *Hôtel du Nord* by French director Marcel Carné, with Arletty and Louis Jouvet playing the title roles.

# CANAL SAINT-MARTIN 55

You can sit back and enjoy a very different aspect of the canal, built between 1805 and 1825, during a two-hour boat trip with a Bateau-Mouche; the trip takes you from the Bassin de la Villette in the north to the Bassin de l'Arsenal, the dock of the Bastille, where the canal enters the Seine.

There are numerous locks and bridges along the Canal Saint-Martin. Freight boats only rarely use the waterway nowadays; you'll see mostly excursion boats instead.

Paris 159

# FURTHER AFIELD

Traditionally, Paris cemeteries were located next to churches in the heart of the city, but as the centuries passed, space ran out. In 1804, Napoleon ordered the construction of three new cemeteries on the edge of the city – Montparnasse, Montmartre, and Père-Lachaise. The latter was created on land that had belonged to the father confessor of Louis XIV, the Jesuit priest Père de La Chaize. Between 1824 and 1850, the cemetery was extended six times and is now the largest in Paris, at 43 hectares (106 acres) Many famous people are buried – or reburied – here, including the dramatist

Many famous personalities have found their last resting place here, such as the Polish composer Frédéric Chopin (above) and Jim Morrison, the lead singer of the Doors who died in 1971 (top right). Other graves are remarkable because of their design (large picture).

160 Paris

# PÈRE-LACHAISE CEMETERY

Molière, the poet Jean de La Fontaine, and Abélard and Héloïse, the tragic 12th-century lovers. More recent interments include Doors singer, Jim Morrison, Edith Piaf, Oscar Wilde, Simone Signoret, and Yves Montand. Maps of the graves are available at kiosks at the cemetery entrance.

Fact and fiction are always linked in the life and death of Edith Piaf. Edith Giovanna Gassion (Piaf is a French colloquialism for "sparrow") was born in 1915 – not on the steps of a house in the Paris suburb of Belleville as legend had it, but in a nearby hospital. Edith Piaf died of cancer in 1963 near Grasse in the south of France, but it is also said that, feeling the "Little Sparrow" should not have died anywhere but in Paris, her husband Théo Sarapo had her body transported illegally to the capital. However, the successes in Edith Piaf's life were not fictional. Often regarded as France's greatest popular singer, she enjoyed huge respect as a performer with her chanson, "*Je ne regrette rien*", which seems to have been her philosophy on life. And who doesn't know "*La vie en rose*", one of the most beautiful love songs of all time? A number of singers have Piaf to thank for a start to

# EDITH PIAF

their careers: Yves Montand, Charles Aznavour, and Georges Moustaki. In 1949 she created a permanent tribute to Paris with her song, "*Paris, tu es ma galeté, Paris, tu es ma douceur aussi, tu es toute ma tendresse.*" ("Paris, you're my joy, Paris, you're my sweetness too, you are my love ".)

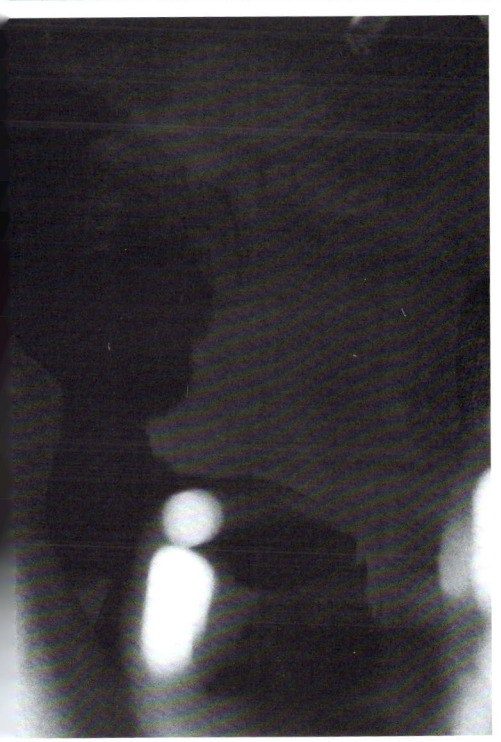

Only 1.47 m (5ft tall), the little "Sparrow of Paris", Edith Piaf, was adored by millions. Yet despite all the adoration she never found the big love of her life, although she continually searched for it. And so many pictures of the singer, who glorified love in her chansons, show her to be, in fact, very lonely.

Paris 163

## FURTHER AFIELD

Parc de la Villette was created in the 1980s, on the site of the huge Parisian slaughterhouse which was closed and cleared in 1974. This science, music, and art complex was designed by architects Bernard Tschumi and Adrian Fainsilber. The park's dominant building is the stunning Cité des Sciences et de l'Industrie, which was opened in 1986 and is Europe's largest science museum. An exhibition space, Explora, features thrilling interactive games, plus information on current scientific developments If you're interested in music, the Cité de la Musique, designed by Christian de Portzam-

# PARC DE LA VILLETTE 57

parc is dedicated to music with concert halls, and exhibitions at Musee de Musique. Some of the charm of the 19th century is conveyed by the Grande Halle, a cast-iron construction dating from 1867, which was converted as a multi-purpose hall and is now used as a venue for trade fairs.

Probably the most stunning structure at the Parc de la Villette is La Géode (large picture), which is located close to the Cité des Sciences et de l'Industrie, together with a museum, planetarium, library, and other institutions. At the opposite end of the park is the Cité de la Musique and its cultural institutions (above).

# FURTHER AFIELD

On December 20, 1996, less than a year after the former President's death, the new Bibliothèque Nationale François Mitterrand library was opened in the up-and-coming district of Tolbiac. About ten million books were moved there from its previous site, near the Palais Royal which was originally opened to the public in 1692. French architect, Dominique Perrault's plans won the competition to design the library which was held in 1988 and he created four angled towers each supposedly representing an open book. The four glazed towers comprise: Tour des

# NATIONAL LIBRARY 58

Temps (Tower of Time), Tour des Lois (Tower of Laws), Tour des Nombres (Tower of Numbers), and Tour des Lettres (Tower of Letters). However, some of the valuable treasures – manuscripts, incunabula, (books printed before 1501), and etchings remain in the previous national library building.

Located immediately beside the Seine in the up-and-coming district of Tolbiac, the towers of the new Bibiothèque Nationale each rise to 79 m (259 ft), (large picture and top). Designed by the architect Dominique Perrault, the façades of the buildings mostly consist of glass (above). In the middle of the complex, is a secluded garden, closed to the public, reminiscent of a medieval cloister.

Paris 167

During his long period in office, François Mitterrand initiated a number of projects that have had a major impact on Paris. In 1981 he instigated the "Grand Louvre" project, in which the Louvre gained its initially controversial but now much-loved glass pyramid, designed by the Chinese-American architect Ieoh Ming Pei. Mitterrand also moved the Finance Ministry out of the Louvre to its own building in Bercy, to create extra exhibition space, and other rooms, such as the Galerie d'Apollon, were renovated. Thanks to Mitterrand, even La Défense – an area that had long been spurned by tourists – became an attraction when the Grande Arche, by the Danish architect Otto von Spreckelsen, was officially opened on July 14 1989, the bicentenary of the French Revolution. On the same day, the Opéra Bastille by the Canadian architect Carlos Ott was also inaugurated – it remained

François Mitterrand (above), the President of France from 1981 to 1995, has left his stamp on the landscape of Paris more than any other French head of state. The glass pyramid is now the most distinctive aspect of the "Grand Louvre" project (large picture). The Opéra Bastille (top right) was inaugurated on the 200th anniversary of the French Revolution.

168 Paris

# MITTERRAND AND HIS BUILDINGS

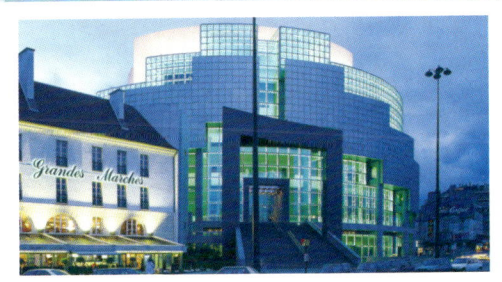

closed for further work until performances began in March 1990. Mitterrand's final major project was the ultra-modern Bibliothèque Nationale François Mitterrand with its four glass-faced towers, but he died in January 1996, almost a year before the enormous project was completed.

Paris 169

Even if you have only little time to explore the surroundings of Paris you should definitely visit the Chateau of Versailles. The Fountain of Apollo (below) is one of the highlights of the palace's park.

# BEYOND PARIS

Paris has so many magnificent sights that you could easily spend a few weeks just exploring the city. Yet there are also some architectural highlights in the surrounding area which are definitely worth seeing. The Basilica of Saint-Denis, for example, an early and venerable example of Gothic design, has been the burial place of French kings for centuries. Vincennes, Fontainebleau, Versailles, and Malmaison, have in their time, all played an important part in history. And when tourists have had their fill of culture, Disneyland Resort Paris can provide alternative entertainment for all the family to enjoy.

# BEYOND PARIS

Versailles is a feast of baroque and the major symbol of the Ancien Régime's system of absolute monarchy. In 1662 Sun King Louis XIV began work on converting a small hunting lodge. He employed the most brilliant craftsmen of the day, including architects Louis Le Vau and Jules Hardouin-Mansart, painter Charles Le Brun, and landscape artist André Le Nôtre, who designed the park. The highlights include the Galerie des Glaces (Hall of Mirrors), the opera house, the Grands Appartements, and the chapel. The gardens epitomize the classic formal French garden design, with geometric

Versailles, in all its glory and with more than 2,000 rooms, was a symbol of corrupt power to the revolutionaries more than anything else. The highlights at the palace are the Hall of Mirrors (large picture), measuring 73 by 11 m (240 by 36 ft), the War Room, and the Palace Theater (above). The entrance gate is also magnificent (top right).

172 Paris

# VERSAILLES 59

flowerbeds and beautiful fountains. Also in the grounds are two small palaces, the Grand and Petit Trianon (the latter built by Louis XV for Madame de Pompadour), the Orangery and the Hameau (hamlet), a collection of rustic houses where the wife of Louis XVI, Marie Antoinette lived.

Crowned King of France at the age of four, Louis XIV (1638 – 1715), known as the Sun King, initially left the business of government to his Cardinal Mazarin, the most powerful man in France since the early death of Louis XIII. When Mazarin, the real father of French absolutism, died in 1661, the 23-year-old king took over the running of the centrally governed and tightly organized state; both nobility and bourgeoisie had been largely disabled in political terms by Mazarin. Louis brought the absolutist system to its climax, until all power was concentrated in him alone: "I am the state", was his motto. In terms of foreign policy, Louis' ambition was the predominance of France in Europe. For decades he conducted war against the Habsburg empire, England, and the Netherlands. And since war has always been the most costly passion of the rulers, more

Above: Louis XIV in his early years, wearing full coronation robes, painting by Justus van Egmont, 1651-1654. Louis XIV loved to show off. The allonge wig he invented (a curly wig down to the shoulders) became an important fashion accessory in Europe during the Baroque period. The portraits by Pierre Mignard (right) and Hyacinthe Rigaud (middle: ready for battle; far right: wearing ermine) also served to glorify the monarch.

174 Paris

# LOUIS XIV

expensive even than any courtly splendor, Louis left a mountain of debts that soon became a long-lasting problem for the country. Louis was succeeded by his five-year old great-grandson who became Louis XV after what still is the longest documented reign of any European monarch.

Born in Paris in 1613, André Le Nôtre, came from a family of gardeners. While he was completing his art studies he was already deeply interested in the design of gardens, and on graduating, he worked at Fontainebleau and in the Tuileries in Paris. His first great independent commission was the park of Chateau Vaux-le-Vicomte, created for Nicolas Fouquet, the finance minister under Louis XIV. The park aroused the envy of the Sun King, who hired the men who had worked on the design to create even more splendid gardens at Versailles. Louis also employed Le Nôtre and the extensive park he created at Versailles was to become his most important creation. Le Nôtre's name became synonymous with classic formal French gardens and his designs were soon imitated throughout Europe. Le Nôtre's work was not only in France, where he also created the gardens of the

The artist and his creations: portrait of André Le Nôtre by the Italian painter Carlo Maratta (above). The park of the Chateau Vaux-le-Vicomte was Le Nôtre's first important commission (top). Of greater importance, though, is the park complex at Versailles with its wonderful water features and delicate detail on the fountains (large picture).

# ANDRÉ LE NÔTRE

chateaux at Chantilly, Meudon, Saint-Cloud, Sceaux, and Chantilly, as well as the terraces of Saint-Germain-en-Laye. In England, he was responsible for the designs of London's Greenwich Park and St James's Park, while in Italy he designed the park of the Villa Torrigiani di Camigliano near Lucca.

# BEYOND PARIS

The origins of the Chateau Malmaison lie in the mists of history, as does the origin of its odd name – "bad house". Malmaison was first documented as the name of an estate in the mid-13th century. It was converted to a chateau in the 18th century, and the interior took on its current form when Joséphine de Beauharnais, wife of the future Emperor Napoleon, acquired the estate in 1799 and carried out renovations. She also had the park redesigned, with hothouses for exotic plants and a well-stocked rose garden. After separating from Napoleon in 1809, she withdrew to Malmaison where she

# MALMAISON 60

lived until her death in 1814. Not all the furniture is from Malmaison; some pieces come from other chateaux where Napoleon lived and only the library has been maintained in its original state. The emperor and his wife are also commemorated in the museum at nearby Château de Bois-Préau.

Today, in the park and the chateau of Malmaison, you can still follow in the footsteps of Napoleon and gain an insight into his personality, for example in his library (large picture). The chateau has remained virtually unchanged, as you can see from the painting by Pierre-Joseph Petit dating from 1805 (top). An unknown artist painted the portrait of Napoleon with the Chateau of Malmaison in the background (above).

# BEYOND PARIS

The Basilica of Saint-Denis lies in the northern suburb of the same name, and can easily be reached by metro or RER. It was constructed in the 12th century under Abbot Suger on the site of a 5th-century chapel. After he was beheaded on Montmartre, Saint Dionysius or Saint Denis supposedly managed to reach this spot carrying his head in his hands. The birthplace of Gothic style, the basilica represents a landmark in architecture. Pointed arches, rib vaulting, rose windows – all the elements that give lightness and air to buildings constructed in this great medieval style were used here

# BASILICA OF SAINT-DENIS 61

for the first time. Saint-Denis – in common with the earlier chapel – is the burial place of all but three French kings up to Louis XVIII. Their magnificent tombs, often bearing effigies of the kings, withstood the Revolution and provide an overview of twelve centuries of French sculptural art.

The Basilica of Saint-Denis (top and above) was the earliest masterpiece in the Gothic style, with the rose window and the skyward striving pillars being two of its most significant characteristics. Many French monarchs found their resting place here, often in magnificently embellished tombs. Large picture: sculptures on the base of the tomb of Louis XII and Anne de Bretagne.

Paris 181

# BEYOND PARIS

In April 1992, Disneyland Paris, officially known as Disneyland Resort Paris, was opened on a 2-hectare (5-acre) site about 30 km (19 miles) to the east of Paris. Following Tokyo in Japan, it was the second Disney resort to open outside the United States. Immerse yourself in a world of make-believe in true American style. Meet Indiana Jones or the Pirates of the Caribbean in Adventureland; visit a Wild West town in Frontierland; shop in Main Street, USA, which reproduces the main street of a small American town at the start of the 20th century; peer into the future in Discoveryland.

# DISNEYLAND PARIS 62

And introduce younger visitors to the charms of characters such as Peter Pan, Sleeping Beauty, and Alice in Wonderland. Opened in 2002, Walt Disney Studios Park has four studio backlots, stages and special effect shows. There is also a wide range of hotels and restaurants to choose from.

With its numerous shops, hotels, and fairground attractions, Marne-la-Vallée, east of Paris, is a perfect area for young and old to visit. One of the most remarkable fantasy structures is the many-turreted Sleeping Beauty castle (large picture).

Paris 183

# BEYOND PARIS

As in many other chateaux, French monarchs left their mark on Fontainebleau. The original Renaissance building, designed by architect Philibert Delorme for François I in 1528, was extended under Henri II, Henri IV, and Louis XV. Arranged around a series of court yards, the interiors were conceived and designed by Italian artists Rosso Fiorentino, Francesco Primaticcio, and Niccolò dell'Abbate, who set the style for the School of Fontainebleau, an elegant version of the Italian Mannerist style. Following a period of decline after the Revolution, the chateau acquired a new grandeur

The chateau of Fontainebleau lies in the heart of an extensive forest of the same name to the south of Paris (large picture). Built for François I, the interior attests to the king's love of art, as can be seen in the long library (above) and the palace chapel (top right).

184 Paris

## FONTAINEBLEAU 63

with renovations carried out under Napoleon. The emperor is believed to have signed his abdication in the Salon Rouge and said goodbye to his Old Guard in the subsequently named Cour des Adieux, before his exile to Elba in 1814. Mementoes are on view in rooms furnished for him in 1808.

The illuminated Eiffel Tower stands out as the tallest structure in the sea of lights that is Paris.

# COMPACT PARIS

Paris has something for everyone – the only difficulty is choosing what to do first! There's no need for children to be bored in this gerat city – there's always a visit to a zoo or a museum of magic, a puppet show, or a dolls' museum, or just using up some energy running around a park. And for adults there is much more to Paris than just museums – you can sample the famous French cuisine, relax while strolling through one of the parks, or while away the time in a street café, watching the world go by. All of this makes Paris, the city of lights and the city of love, shine and sparkle in all the shades of the rainbow.

# COMPACT PARIS

*The Comédie Française tends to perform classic French drama.*

## MUSEUMS, MUSIC, DRAMA

### Comédie Française
The Comédie-Française was founded in 1680 by King Louis XIV. Originally based on the Rive Gauche, in Rue de l'Ancienne Comédie in the heart of the Latin Quarter, it has been performing here at the Place Colette since 1807. The Comédie Française is the only national theater in France with its own troupe of actors; it concentrates primarily on staging French classics.
*1 place Colette, 75001,*
*Tel 42 60 03 16,*
*www.comedie-francaise.fr*

### Maison Européenne de la Photographie
The City of Paris renovated and converted the interior of a palace dating from 1706 to provide a home for this institution dedicated to contemporary photography. In addition to permanent exhibitions, there are temporary exhibitions showing works by well-known photographers. There is also a library, a video library, and a lecture hall.
*5/7 rue de Fourcy, 75004,*
*Tel 44 78 75 00,*
*www.mep-fr.org,*
*Wed–Sun 11.00–20.00.*

### Musée National de l'Orangerie
The core of the collection of renowned art dealer Paul Guillaume is on display in the Orangerie, close to the Place de la Concorde. This is an outstanding collection of works by classic modern artists such as Paul Cézanne, Auguste Renoir, Henri Rousseau, Henri Matisse, Amedeo Modigliani, Marie Laurencin, Pablo Picasso, André Derain, and Maurice Utrillo. The works by these masters alone make a visit to the museum worthwhile, but the highlight of the Orangerie is located in the basement – two rooms displaying the *Nymphéas*, the huge Impressionist water-lily paintings that Claude Monet spent almost 30 years of his life painting.
*Place de la Concorde, 75001,*
*Tel 42 97 48 16,*
*9.45–17.00, daily.*

### Olympia
Constructed in 1888, the Olympia is the oldest music hall in Paris still in existence. Over the course of the decades, all the stars of French show business have appeared here, including Edith Piaf, Georges Brassens, Charles Aznavour, Juliette Gréco, Gilbert Bécaud, Johnny Halliday, Sylvie Vartan, to name just a few; many of the great international stars have appeared here too, such as Louis Armstrong, Frank Sinatra, Ray Charles, Bob Dylan, the Beatles, and the Rolling

# ÎLE DE LA CITÉ, RIVE DROITE

The Maison Européenne de la Photographie focuses on modern photography.

Stones. The Olympia still draws the big names today – if you are asked to appear at the Olympia, you really know you've made it.
*28 boulevard des Capucines, 75001, Tel 08 92 68 33 68, www.olympiahall.com*

### Théâtre du Châtelet
The Théâtre du Châtelet was officially opened in the presence of Empress Eugénie in August 1862. With 2,500 seats, it is one of the largest theatrical venues in Paris. In addition to drama, music has played an important role here – in 1873, French conductor Edouard Colonne introduced the Concerts Colonne, attracting some of the greatest composers of the time to Paris: Tchaikovsky, Grieg, Richard Strauss, Debussy. In 1913 the venue experienced the greatest scandal in French theatrical history when Igor Stravinsky's ballet *Le Sacre du Printemps* was premiered here. The Théâtre du Châtelet does not have a resident company but hosts guest performances of operas, ballets, musicals, and concerts.
*1 place du Châtelet, 75001, Tel 40 28 28 40, www.theatre-chatelet.com*

### Théâtre du Palais Royal
Not far from the Comédie-Française, this theater was commissioned by Cardinal Richelieu in the east wing of his residence, the Palais Royal. Today the venue is predominantly dedicated to light entertainment. Film fans may recognize the building from the film *Charade* starring Audrey Hepburn and Cary Grant. It formed the backdrop for the film's exciting climax. If you have the chance, stroll through the building during the interval to admire the grand interiors of the foyer, corridors, and stairways.
*38 rue Montpensier, 75001, Tel 42 97 40 00, www.theatrepalaisroyal.com*

## FESTIVALS AND EVENTS

### Fête des Tuileries
A large funfair has been held in the gardens of the Tuileries every August since 1985. There are modern fairground rides and more traditional carousels, and other classic rides such as the dodgems, plus plenty of amusements for families, and kiosks selling fast food and drink. Reaching high into the sky and looking very spectacular at night, the big wheel can be seen from a distance.
*August, Sun–Thurs 12.00–24.00; Fri, Sat 12.00–1.00.*

### Paris Plages
Parts of the right bank of the Seine are covered with truckloads of sand every summer, transporting Parisians to the

Paris 189

# COMPACT PARIS

Paris Plages: vacation in the middle of the big city.

seaside for a few weeks in July and August. Sports are also catered for, with a crazy golf course and an area devoted to fitness. Temporary beaches are installed in other locations too, such as on the Bassin de la Villette and on the Seine near the new Bibliothèque nationale.
*At the Voie Georges Pompidou from Pont Marie to the Pont de Sully, 75004, www.paris.fr/portail/ete, Mid-July to mid-August.*

**Finish of the Tour de France**
Since 1975 the final stage of Tour de France – the most difficult of cycle races demanding feats of strength – has always ended on the Champs-Élysées in Paris. All the roads in the nearby area are closed to traffic as the cyclists make their way along the final part of the route, up the Rue de Rivoli, the Voie Georges Pompidou, through the Place de la Concorde. The roads are lined by thousands of spectators, cheering on their rider or team.
*Avenue des Champs-Élysées, 75008, www.letour.fr, End of July.*

SPORT, GAMES, FUN

**Musée de la Curiosité et de la Magie**
This is where the enchanting world of magic from the 18th century to the present day comes to life. It also has a school of magic, as well as a gift shop selling items related to magic. The museum has already received several "unusual museum" awards.
*11 rue Saint-Paul, 75004, Tel 42 72 13 26, www.museedelamagie.com, Wed, Sat, Sun 14.00–19.00.*

**Musée de la Poupée**
Some 500 dolls are on display here, made from porcelain, paper, celluloid, or plastic, dating from 1800 to the present day and mainly of French origin. In addition to the permanent collection, the museum holds exhibitions devoted to related subjects. There is also a shop selling handmade dolls, soft toys, and books. And very important for the mummies of dolls – there's also a dolls' hospital.
*Impasse Berthaud, 75003, Tel 42 72 73 11, www.museedelapoupeeparis.com, Tues–Sun 10.00–18.00.*

**Piscine Suzanne Berlioux**
This modern indoor Olympic-sized swimming pool is located in the Forum des Halles shopping area, on the site of the former market halls. A glasshouse with tropical plants completes this oasis of calm in the heart of the city.
*Forum des Halles, 10 place de la Rotonde,*

190 Paris

# ÎLE DE LA CITÉ, RIVE DROITE

Paris is the dream destination of each cyclist – to watch the final stage of the Tour de France.

*Tel 42 36 98 44,*
*Mon, Tues 11.30–22.00, Wed 10.00–22.00, Thurs, Fri 11.00–22.00, Sat, Sun 9.00–19.00.*

## SHOPPING

### Au Nain Bleu
The largest toy store in Paris has been making children's dreams come true for over 150 years. Even the store itself seems to have emerged from the midst of a dream, as the home of the Blue Dwarf – in French, the Nain Bleu – is designed as a circus tent. There are elaborate toys at very high prices, but also some cheaper items as well. A good place to buy gifts, or to keep them entertained if another museum seems too much to bear.
*5 boulevard Malesherbes, 75008, Tel 42 65 20 00, www.aunainbleu.com, Mon 14.00–19.00, Tues–Sat 10.00–19.00.*

### Bazar de l'Hôtel de Ville
Abbreviated to BHV, this is one of the oldest department stores in Paris. The range of goods includes clothing, books, and gifts, and everything you need for the home – it is a paradise for DIYers in particular.
*52–64 rue de Rivoli, 75004, Tel 42 74 90 00, www.bhv.fr, Mon–Sat 9.30–19.30, Wed until 21.00.*

### Centre Commercial du Carrousel du Louvre
Below ground level, and part of the Louvre complex, this elegant but expensive shopping mall has 35 shops offering a wide range of goods: from fashion and cosmetics, glass and porcelain, to books and CDs in the Virgin Megastore. There's also a patisserie and a food court, offering dishes from around the world: Spanish, Italian, Asian, Lebanese, Moroccan, North and South American, and, of course, French cuisine. If you tire of shopping and prefer a little culture, there is the Studio Théâtre of the Comédie-Française.
*Le Carrousel du Louvre, 99 rue de Rivoli, 75001, Tel 43 16 47 10, www.carrouseldulouvre.com, shops are open from 10.00–20.00; restaurants from 8.00–23.00.*

### Chanel Joaillerie
Almost every building in the Place Vendôme is home to a world-famous company, such as Chanel, which also presents its jewelry collection here. Many of the items on sale reflect the designs of the legendary Coco Chanel.
*18 place Vendôme, 75001, Tel 55 35 50 05, www.chanel.com, Mon–Sat 11:00–19:00.*

# COMPACT PARIS

**Hermès is a brand of unadulterated luxury in fashion.**

### Galerie Véro-Dodat
Home to a variety of different shops and with an elegant atmosphere, the covered Parisian arcades and galleries, the oldest of which is Galerie Véro-Dodat dating from 1826, were in effect shopping malls long before the term was invented. Many of the old, decorative wooden store façades have been preserved. In addition to a café, there is also a store selling wonderful old dolls, a leatherware store, and a cosmetic store, among others.
*From 19 rue Jean-Jacques Rousseau to 2 rue du Bouloi, 75001.*

### Hermès
The history of the Hermès company dates back to 1837, when the saddler Thierry Hermès opened his first store in Paris. Toward the end of the 19th century, the company moved to the Faubourg Saint-Honoré, where it is still based. The range was soon expanded to include cases and leather bags; then the famous silk scarves arrived. There have been Hermès perfumes since the 1960s, and a range of prêt-à-porter clothing was introduced in the 1980s.
*24 faubourg Saint-Honoré, 75008, Tel 40 17 47 17, www.hermes.com, Mon–Sat 10.30–18.30.*

## EATING AND DRINKING

### Au Pied de Cochon
This restaurant is a last remnant from the great era of market halls. When Les Halles was still in existence, suppliers came here for a hearty meal at the crack of dawn before returning home, followed later on by the market traders. A good, solid cuisine is still on offer today, and the restaurant is open around the clock; the menu is based on meat, mainly pork, as indicated by the name *Au Pied de Cochon* (*The Pig's Trotter*).
*6 rue Coquillière, 75001, Tel 40 13 77, www.pieddecochon.com, around the clock, daily.*

### Café de la Paix
In the lavishly decorated dining room – or even better – on the terrace in the summer guests may enjoy traditonal French cooking with an intersting modern twist.
*5 place de l'Opéra, 75002, Tel 40 07 36 36, 7.00–0.30, daily.*

### Café Marly
The great plus point of this café is its outstanding position. Situated beneath the arcades of the Louvre, its customers are transported back to the time of the emperor Napoleon III. And when the tables and chairs are

**192 Paris**

# ÎLE DE LA CITÉ, RIVE DROITE

**At the Café Marly you can observe the Louvre from close up.**

set out in the courtyard in sunny weather, with a direct view of the large Glass Pyramid of the Louvre, you might also be able to forget the rather steep prices that are charged here for coffee and tea.
*93 rue de Rivoli, cour Napoléon im Louvre, 75001,*
*Tel 49 26 06 60,*
*8.00–2.00, daily.*

## Fauchon
Whether you come for breakfast, for a lunchtime meal, or for dinner, the café belonging to the internationally renowned delicatessen store offers the perfect choice of dishes at any time.
*30 place de la Madeleine, 75008, Tel 70 39 38 39,*
*Mon–Sat 9.00–23.00.*

## L'Ambroisie
Illustrious guests on state visits have been brought to the L'Ambroisie, one of the most renowned restaurants in Paris. Located in one of the typical houses lining the Place des Vosges, the building resembles an Italian palazzo. The chef Bernard Pacaud serves dishes according to what is in season in his restaurant, which has received three Michelin stars. The wine list offers a correspondingly rich selection of the best vintages.
*9 place des Vosges, 75004,*
*Tel 42 78 51 45, www. ambroisieplacedesvosges.com, Tues–Sat 12.00–13.30, 20.00–21.30.*

## Le Souk
Passing through the entrance lined with olive trees, you would think you were in North Africa. The furnishings suit the Moroccan cuisine served here. The menu includes many couscous and tagine dishes, as well as grilled meats and also vegetarian options. Even the wine comes from North Africa – some are from Algeria, others from Morocco; but French and European wines are, of course, also on offer.
*1 rue Keller, 75011,*
*Tel 49 29 05 08,*
*www.lesoukfr.com*

## Maxim's
This legendary restaurant can look back over an illustrious hundred years of history as a meeting place for the rich and beautiful. The original furnishings are still preserved. They were finished in time for the World Exhibition in 1900 – and you can see art nouveau style in its most lavish and exquisite form here. Wall decorations, doors, multi-hued glass windows all work together beautifully and bring the past to life.
*3 rue Royale, 75008,*
*Tel 42 65 27 94,*
*www.maxims-de-paris.com,*
*Mon–Sat 19.00–22.30.*

# COMPACT PARIS

The Hôtel Caron de Beaumarchais allows you to indulge in Louis-Seize-style luxury.

### Zen
This very modern restaurant is mainly decorated in white, with chairs forming a vivid contrast. There is a huge selection of traditional Japanese dishes, which go down well with the many Japanese guests who come here – a indication of its authentic cuisine.
*8, rue de l'Echelle, 75001, Tel 42 61 93 99, www.restaurant-zen.fr.cc, 12.00–15.00, 19.00–22.30, daily.*

## ACCOMMODATION

### Hôtel Caron de Beaumarchais
The poet Beaumarchais wrote his *Marriage of Figaro* in this building. An attempt has been made to recreate the atmosphere of that time with furnishings that include an Erard piano from 1792, a Louis XVI fireplace, and antique candleholders. The hotel rooms are also decorated in the same style, but without sacrificing modern comforts such as televisions and Internet access.
*12 rue Vieille-du-Temple, 75004, Tel 42 72 34 12, www.carondebeaumarchais.com*

### Hotel des Deux-Îles
This beautiful hotel, with rooms decorated in discreet modern tones, lies at the heart of the Île Saint-Louis. The age of the building is, however, apparent in the lounge. On cold evenings, guests can sit by the open fire under the vaulted ceiling. The hotel's position on the island, means the location is quiet, but just a short distance to the Latin Quarter.
*59 rue Saint-Louis-en-l' Île, 75004, Tel 43 26 13 35, www.deuxiles-paris-hotel.com*

### Hôtel de la Bretonnerie
This old palace of the nobility, with its 29 guest rooms, is located not far from the Place des Vosges in the Marais. Each room is individually designed, and all are tastefully in keeping with the style of the building. Even if the exposed beams might remind you of times past, the high-tech facilities and internet access on offer will meet your every need.
*22 rue Sainte-Croix de la Bretonnerie, 75004, Tel 48 87 77 63, www.hotelbretonnerie.com*

### Hôtel du Cygne
If you would like to reach most of the Parisian attractions on foot, then you should consider this hotel. Its position right by the Centre Pompidou makes it an ideal starting point for expeditions. The hotel has a total of 19 rooms and one suite. In the attractive breakfast room,

# ÎLE DE LA CITÉ, RIVE DROITE

*The famous Bluebell Girls, long-legged dancers of the Lido, are the hallmark of the revue venue.*

images of the eponymous swan as in the hotel's name dominate the scene.
*3–5 rue du Cygne, 75001,*
*Tel 42 60 14 16,*
*www.cygne-hotel-paris.com*

### Hôtel Madeleine-Opéra
At first sight and judging from the façade, it appears that this is one of those sweet, old-fashioned, wooden-clad Parisian shops, but when you look more closely, you realize it's a hotel – and not only that: it's also relatively affordable for one of the most expensive districts of Paris. The rooms are simple and elegant; breakfast is served in the room.
*12 rue Greffulhe, 75008,*
*Tel 47 42 26 26.*

## NIGHTLIFE

### Andy Wahloo
Wahloo means "I have nothing", in Arabic and yet this bar and nightclub venue seems to have a lot to offer with a very unusual decor that is based upon North African pop with an Andy Warhol twist. Early in the evening, the Moroccan tapas served here may still be the focus of all the attention. But the DJs are certain to liven up the atmosphere on the dance floor later in the evening, or you can relax and enjoy a mojito or two.
*69 rue des Gravilliers, 75003,*
*Tel 42 71 20 38,*
*Tues–Sun 17.00–2.00.*

### Crazy Horse Saloon
The shows staged at this cabaret, founded in 1951, are considered to be the most daring in the whole of Paris. Dancers of similar height and build are chosen to give a uniform look to the line-up, although in terms of their costume it is more a question of clever lighting than fabulous creations. No food is served in the Crazy Horse itself, but there are several first-class restaurants in the area offering a dîner that can be booked in combination with the show.
*12 avenue Georges V, 75008,*
*Tel 47 23 32 32,*
*www.crazyhorse.fr,*
*Mon–Fri, Sun 20.30, 23.00,*
*Sat 19.30, 21.45, 23.50.*

### Le Lido
The sumptuous themed shows, performed by the resident dancers, the Bluebell Girls, with their perfect figures and frequent changes of spectacular costume and clever special effects entertain audiences at the Lido. A special plus for tourists is that you get a perfect view of the show from every seat in the auditorium.
*116 bis avenue des Champs-Élysées, 75008,*
*Tel 40 76 36 10, www.lido.fr,*
*21.30, 22.30, daily.*

# COMPACT PARIS

Musée du Luxembourg is a magnificent building in which you can enjoy great art.

## MUSEUMS, MUSIC, DRAMA

### Musée du Luxembourg
This museum located in the Luxembourg Gardens stages special exhibitions dedicated to the art of the 20th century and of the Renaissance, the era during which Queen Consort Maria de' Medici – the second wife of French King Henri IV – commissioned the creation of the Luxembourg Palace and its magnificent gardens.
*19 rue de Vaugirard, 75006,*
*Tel 42 44 25 95,*
*www.museeduluxembourg.fr,*
*Mon, Fri 10.30–22.00,*
*Tues–Thurs, Sat 10.30–19.00,*
*Sun 9.00–19.00.*

### Muséum National d'Histoire Naturelle
The Jardin des Plantes, the botanical garden founded in 1626 under Louis XIII and opened to the public in 1640, houses the French national natural history museum. It displays exhibits in several different pavilions from geology, mineralogy, and anatomy, as well as fossils and insects. The most interesting part for younger visitors is the Grande Galerie de l'Evolution, where there are stuffed giraffes and lions, and the skeleton of a whale. The development of the species is presented via interactive exhibits, plus nature workshops for children under 12.
*36 rue Geoffroy Saint-Hilaire, 75005, Tel 40 79 54 79,*
*www.mnhn.fr,*
*Wed–Mon 10.00–18.00.*

### Musée Zadkine
The Russian sculptor Ossip Zadkine lived and worked here from 1928 until his death in 1967. When his wife, the artist Valentine Prax, died in 1981, she bequeathed the house and studio along with his personal collection to the City of Paris. The museum was opened in 1982 and in addition to the works of Zadkine, it also stages regular exhibitions of contemporary art.
*100 bis, rue d'Assas, 75006,*
*55 42 77 20,*
*www.zadkine.paris.fr,*
*Tues–Sun 10.00–18.00.*

### L'Odéon – Théâtre de l'Europe
The first theater built on this site was inaugurated in 1782, but in 1799, it was largely destroyed by fire and subsequently restored. In 1958, the revered French actor and director, Jean-Louis Barrault was appointed resident director here. His tenure lasted until 1968 when the building was occupied by students, and he was dismissed. Known as the Théâtre de l'Europe since 1990, the Odéon's repertoire mainly covers the classics, both traditional and modern,

# RIVE GAUCHE, QUARTIER LATIN

L'Odéon – Théâtre de l'Europe can look back on a great past.

frequently performed in other European languages with French subtitles.
*2 rue Corneille, 75006,*
*Tel 44 85 40 00,*
*www.theatre-odeon.fr*

### Théâtre de la Huchette
Founded in 1948, this small, cozy venue was the cradle of the Theater of the Absurd. Some of the most important works by Eugène Ionesco, Jacques Audiberti, Jean Tardieu, and Jean Genet were premiered here. Ionesco's *La Cantatrice Chauve* (*The Bald Soprano*) and *La Leçon* (*The Lesson*) have been performed continuously since 1957, a world record.
*23 rue de la Huchette, 75005,*
*Tel 43 26 38 99,*
*www.theatre-huchette.com*

### Théâtre du Vieux Colombier
Founded in 1913 the Théâtre du Vieux Colombier was threatened with closure in 1975, but thanks to protests and demonstrations by the actors it was saved. In 1986, it was acquired by the City of Paris; today it forms a part of the Comédie Française. Modern plays, both classics and new, are performed here.
*21 rue du Vieux-Colombier, 75006, Tel 44 39 87 00,*
*www.vieux.colombier.free.fr*

## FESTIVALS AND EVENTS

### Paris Cinéma
This film festival takes place every year in July at more than a dozen locations in the city, over one-third of which are in the Latin Quarter. The festival includes a wide list of films from around the world. Internationally famous actors and directors are invited as special guests and add extra glitz and sparkle to the occasion.
*www.pariscinema.org*

### Foire Saint-Germain
For the past 30 years, from late May to early July, this street fair has been staged amid the busy Place Saint-Sulpice. There are special themed markets, including a medieval market, a market for book-lovers, and a ceramics market. The fair also boasts exhibitions, concerts, and drama – some held in the open air and some staged in the Saint-Germain auditorium or in the Saint-Sulpice church itself. There is also plenty to keep children amused.
*www.foiresaintgermain.org*

## SPORT, GAMES, FUN

### Les Marionnettes du Luxembourg
A Théâtre des Marionnettes has been entertaining children at the Jardin du Luxembourg since 1881; the current building dates from 1933. The shows include traditional fairy

# COMPACT PARIS

The Bouquiniste stalls next to the Seine are the place where you might find that antiquarian book or map you are looking for.

tales, such as *Le Chat Botté* (*Puss in Boots*) – suitable for children from two years old.
*Jardin du Luxembourg, 86 rue Notre-Dame des Champs, 75006, Tel 43 26 46 47, www.evene.fr/culture/agenda/marionnettes-du-Luxembourg-3617.php, Wed 15.15, Sat, Sun 11.00, 15.15.*

### Pétanque in the Arènes
Every afternoon and early evening, when the weather permits, players of pétanque, a form of boules, meet here. Many players are members of clubs and take part in the Paris championships each year.
*Arènes de Lutèce, 51 rue Monge, 75005, www.arenesdelutece.com*

### Tennis in the Jardin du Luxembourg
The six tennis courts in the elegant Jardin du Luxembourg are open to the public. The courts have to be booked in advance; the opening times are the same as the park and vary according to the season.
*Jardin du Luxembourg, 75006, Tel 43 25 79 18.*

## SHOPPING

### Bouquinistes
The first bouquinistes began to appear at the start of the 19th century along the banks of the Seine. When the weather is dry, the stallholders (bouquin means 'book') unlock the large, green, oblong boxes that have now become such a typical sight in Paris, especially on the left bank. Book lovers will enjoy browsing through the display second-hand books, old engravings, postcards, and small gifts.
*On the Left Bank of the Seine from the Quai de la Tournelle to the Quai Voltaire, on the Right Bank from Pont Marie to the Quai du Louvre.*

### Mariage Frères
Yes, there really is a French tea-drinking culture in Paris. This is the place if you want to discover its more sophisticated side. The Mariage brothers specialized in importing tea in the mid-19th century. The current owners also offer their customers hand-picked teas of the finest quality. Everything is here, whether you prefer green or black tea, including rare and more unusual teas from India, Sri Lanka, China, Taiwan, Japan, or Africa. They also sell teapots and tea services.
*13 rue des Grands-Augustins, 75006, Tel 40 51 82 50, www.mariagefreres.com, 10.30–19.30, daily.*

### L'Occitane en Provence
Lavender, olives, almonds, lemons – natural products

# RIVE GAUCHE, QUARTIER LATIN

Top-quality tea varieties from around the world can be found at Mariage Frères.

grown in Provence, as well as the oils and fragrances derived from them – are the most important components of the beauty care products and perfumes from L'Occitane. The company has been producing its popular natural cosmetics range for more than 30 years in the small town of Volx near Manosque in Haute-Provence.
*130 rue Mouffetard, 75005, Tel 43 31 98 12, http://fr1.loccitane.com, Mon–Sat 10.30–19.30.*

### Petit Bateau
Delightful clothing for babies and children, made to a very high standard of quality and durability, so it can also withstand a thing or two, is sold at Petit Bateau. The company's slogan is "Des vêtements faits pour faire des choses dedans" (clothes made for doing things in) for good reason. And so the parents don't feel left out, there's also a range of underwear, nightwear, and t-shirts for grown-ups.
*26 rue Vavin, 75006, Tel 55 42 02 53, www.petit-bateau.com, Mon–Sat 10.00–19.00.*

### Shakespeare & Company
There has been an English language bookstore in Paris since 1919. The original store, opened by American Sylvia Beach, soon became a meeting place for literary greats such as F. Scott Fitzgerald, Ernest Hemingway, and James Joyce. In addition to a rich selection of books in English, the store also hosts events such as readings by authors and workshops. Backpackers can sleep upstairs, in return for working in the shop below.
*37 rue de la Bûcherie, 75005, Tel 43 25 40 93, www.shakespeareco.org, 10.00–23.00, daily.*

### Skripta
Lovers of elegant paper and stationery could easily go on a spending spree in this stationer's. There is a wide selection on offer; from calendars, lavishly designed notebooks, top quality fountain pens, boxes of crayons, and painting equipment for children.
*68 rue du Cardinal Lemoine, 75005, Tel 46 33 58 38, www.skripta-paris.com, Tues–Sat 14.00–20.00.*

### Sonia Rykiel
French fashion designer Sonia Rykiel initially made her name with her fashion knitwear. Today she provides a broadly diverse range of fashions for men and women, as well as cosmetics. Other shops are located in the Rue de Grenelle.
*175 boulevard Saint-Germain, 75006, Tel 49 54 60 60, www.soniarykiel.com, Mon–Sat 10.30–19.00.*

# COMPACT PARIS

The elegant La Tour d'Argent restaurant offers exquisite food as well as superb views of the Seine and Notre-Dame.

## EATING AND DRINKING

### Huîtrerie Régis
A little bit of real heaven for gourmets: delicious oysters, delivered fresh from the oyster beds of the Marennes d'Oléron in the Atlantic. Enjoy your oysters with a glass of wine in a pleasant, intimate atmosphere. What more could an oyster-lover want?
*3 rue de Montfaucon, 75006, Tel 44 41 10 07, www.huitrerieregis.com, Tues–Sun 11.00–24.00, closed mid-July to Sept.*

### L'Atelier de Joël Robuchon
One of the restaurants owned by Joël Robuchon, one of the best-known chefs in France. In 2008, the Atelier was awarded a second star by the Michelin food critics.
*5 rue de Montalembert, 75007, Tel 01 42 22 56 56, 11.30–15.30, 18.30–24.00, daily.*

### La Bastide Odéon
The elegant Mediterranean ambience of this restaurant with its warm tones brings out the holiday atmosphere; the dishes are highly evocative of the warmth of the south of France. Fresh vegetables, fish, and seafood fetaure on the menu. The wines come mainly from areas in the south of France, such as Provence and Languedoc- Roussillon.
*7 rue Corneille, 75006, Tel 43 26 03 65, www.bastide-odeon.com, Tues–Sat 12.15–14.00, 19.30–22.30.*

### Les Deux Magots
A café that awards a prize for literature? Where else but in Paris could this happen? Since 1933, the greats of literature and art have enjoyed their coffee in the Deux Magots: Picasso, André Gide, Ernest Hemingway, Simone de Beauvoir, Jean-Paul Sartre, among many others. Today the Deux Magots is mostly frequented by tourists in search of a piece of Bohemia; the prices reflect the café's illustrious reputation.
*6 place Saint-Germain-des-Prés, 75006, Tel 45 48 55 25, 7.30–1.00, daily.*

### Jardin Notre-Dame
Although this restaurant is just a few steps from the tourist attractions, it offers excellent traditional French cuisine at moderate prices. In addition, you get a fantastic view of Notre-Dame, free of charge, from the terrace in summer.
*2 rue du Petit Pont, 75005, Tel 43 54 03 75, 12.00–14.30, 19.00–24.00, daily.*

### La Tour d'Argent
This restaurant is a real legend. Kings and emperors, film stars, and politicians – just about

# RIVE GAUCHE, QUARTIER LATIN

*Le Train Bleu is the place to dine surrounded by lavish gold decor.*

everyone who was or is anyone – has been a guest here. The restaurant is mainly known for its duck dishes. Raised on the restaurant's own farm, each duck is given its own serial number, which the guest who has enjoyed it can take home as a memento. Thanks to its prime location on the fifth floor, over-looking the Seine, the restaurant enjoys a wonderful view over the islands. But check your wallet is well stocked before making a reservation. Men must wear ties in the evening.
*15/17 quai de la Tournelle, 75005, Tel 43 54 23 31, www.tourdargent.com, Wed–Sun 12.00–13.30, 19.30–21.00, Tues 19.30–21.00.*

## Le Train Bleu

The main focus of attention in this restaurant is not the – admittedly excellent – food but the surroundings in which it is eaten. The Paris-Lyon-Méditerranée railway company had the restaurant established here for the World Exhibition of 1900, in the hall of the station from which trains depart for the south. It was originally called the Buffet de la Gare de Lyon, but in 1963 was renamed after the legendary Train Bleu. The décor is highly ornate with gilded carvings and more than 50 paintings decorating the walls, mainly showing the destinations of the trains that departed from here.
*On the upper floor of the Gare de Lyon, place Louis Armand, 75012, Tel 44 75 76 76, www.le-train-bleu.com, 11.30–15.00, 19.00–23.00, daily.*

## Le Ziryab

Located on the top floor of the Institut du Monde Arabe, this restaurant serves Moroccan cuisine with an international twist. In fine weather, when Arabian delicacies and refreshing thé à la menthe are also served on the roof terrace, look out to see the heart of Paris at your feet.
*1 rue des Fossés Saint-Bernard, 75005, Tel 55 42 55 42, www.imarabe.org/restaurant.html, Tues–Sat 11.00–23.30, Sun 11.00–14.30.*

## ACCOMMODATION

### Grand Hôtel des Balcons

In one of the small streets between the Boulevard Saint-Germain and the Jardin du Luxembourg, this hotel offers 50 quiet, cozy rooms, which also provide satellite TV and Internet connections. For what is a typical French hotel, the breakfast buffet is unusually lavish, with bread, jams, cakes, fruit, different egg dishes, fried potatoes, and baked beans.

# COMPACT PARIS

Bars and bistros are well frequented late into the night.

3 rue Casimir Delavigne, 75006, Tel 46 34 78 50, www.hotelgrandsbalcons.com

## Hôtel de l'Abbaye Saint-Germain

This hotel in a lovely, peaceful location offers not only 44 luxuriously appointed rooms but it also has a few extra comforts such as a television room and a reading room. But, best of all, in summer you can take afternoon tea in the small courtyard garden, and in winter in front of a crackling open fire. Many major attractions such as the Musée d'Orsay, Notre-Dame, and the Louvre can be easily reached on foot.

10 rue Cassette, 75006, Tel 45 44 38 11, www.hotelabbayeparis.com

## Hôtel de Nesle

A small 20-room hotel with charming rooms decorated with murals on a theme or depicting historical events, such as tales from ancient Egypt, the tragic story of Héloïse and Abélard, or scenes inspired by the works of Molière. Some of the rooms offer a view of the charming small garden, and if you want to relax after a strenuous day of sightseeing, the hotel has its own Turkish bath. Room reservations can only be made by phone.

7, rue de Nesle, 75006, Tel 43 54 62 41, www.hoteldenesleparis.com

## Hôtel des Grandes Écoles

This enchanting oasis, with its 51 rooms featuring rustic and cozy furnishings, is located in the heart of Paris, not very far from the hectic hustle and bustle of the boulevards Saint-Michel and Saint-Germain. In summer in particular, when breakfast is served in the small garden, you'll feel like a guest in a French country house miles from the big city.

75 rue Cardinal Lemoine, 75005, Tel 43 26 79 32, www.hotel-grandes-ecoles.com

## Hôtel les Degrés de Notre-Dame

This small, affordable hotel lies just a stone's throw from Notre-Dame, in a street on the Left Bank of the Seine. Of the ten rooms, decorated by the owners with paintings from their private collection, two have a direct view of the cathedral from their windows. However, there is a surcharge for this treat.

10 rue des Grands-Degrés, 75005, Tel 55 42 88 88, www.lesdegreshotel.fr

## Hôtel Lutetia

Built in 1910, this was the first art deco hotel in the city and, even today, guests feel trans-

# RIVE GAUCHE, QUARTIER LATIN

The Quartier Latin is famous for its buzzing nightlife.

ported to the elegance of the belle époque. Many famous names appear on the list of prominent visitors, including the painter Henri Matisse, the writer Antoine de Saint-Exupéry, and the dancer, singer, and actor, Josephine Baker. General de Gaulle even spent his honeymoon in the hotel. In spite of the belle époque flair, the rooms are equipped with every modern detail you might expect. There are two restaurants, a bar, and a fitness room available to hotel guests.
*45 boulevard Raspail,
Tel 49 54 46 46,
www.lutetia-paris.com*

## NIGHTLIFE

### Le Cinéma du Panthéon
Le Cinéma du Panthéon Jean-Paul Sartre and Jacques Prévert often visited this venue. The oldest continuously run cinema in Paris enjoyed a facelift for its 100th birthday. The renovation and redesign – by Catherine Deneuve, together with the set designer Christian Sapet – of the auditorium has provided a salon in which you can enjoy drinks and snacks. The cinema focuses on contemporary French films.
*13 rue Victor-Cousin, 75005,
Tel 40 46 01 21,
www.cinemapantheon.com,
Salon: Mon–Fri 12.00–19.00.*

### Le Mezzanine de l'Alcazar
The Mezzanine, in the Alzazar Restaurant, provides a bar with a great selection of drinks and cocktails, as well as excellent meals, eaten in deep, soft armchairs at small tables. From Friday to Sunday, musical entertainment is provided by some of the best DJs in Paris.
*62 rue Mazarine, 75006,
Tel 53 10 19 99,
www.alcazar.fr,
19.00–2.00, daily.*

### Studio des Ursulines
This cinema, opened in 1926, started its life screening avant-garde films. For the first performance, artists such as André Breton, Man Ray, René Clair, and Fernand Léger were in the audience. Even today, the cinema mainly screens art films outside the mainstream. The cinema is also a venue for the city film festivals.
*10, rue des Ursulines, 75005,
Tel 56 81 15 20,
www.studiodesursulines.com*

### Wagg
A trendy club in the same building as the Mezzanine de l'Alcazar. And where at the weekends, stressed Parisians dance away the tensions of the working week to house, funk, disco, and salsa.
*62 rue Mazarine, 75006,
Tel 55 42 22 00, www.wagg.fr,
Fri, Sat 11.30–6.00,
Sun 15.00–24.00.*

# COMPACT PARIS

The Musée Maillol showcases the artistic work of the sculptor Aristide Maillol.

## MUSEUMS, MUSIC, DRAMA

### Musée des Égouts de Paris
The Quai d'Orsay is the entry point from where you can visit around 500 m (547 yards) of the over 2,000-km (1,250-mile) long network of sewers. The first underground sewer was laid in Napoleon's time. There is also an exhibition on the history of the sewerage system in Paris and solutions for the future.
*Entrance opposite 93 Quai d'Orsay, 75007,*
*Tel 47 05 10 29,*
*summer Sat–Wed 11.00–17.00,*
*winter Sat–Wed 11.00–16.00.*

### Musée Maillol
The Musée Maillol provides an insight into the creative range of sculptor Aristide Maillol, with a comprehensive overview of the whole of his work. There are examples of his art, paintings, and ceramics. You can also see Maillol's personal collection, plus works by Matisse, Degas, Picasso, Ingres, Cézanne, Duchamps, and Kandinsky.
*59–61 rue de Grenelle, 75007,*
*Tel 42 22 59 58,*
*Wed–Mon 18.00.*

### Musée Marmottan Monet
From its very inception, this museum has always been devoted to Impressionism, a focus that was strengthened when Michel Monet, the second son of the painter Claude Monet, bequeathed a series of works to the museum in 1966. Of particular importance is the painting by Monet that gave the whole movement its name: *Impression, soleil levant* (*Impression, Sunrise*).
*2 rue Louis-Boilly, 75016,*
*Tel 44 96 50 33,*
*www.marmottan.com,*
*11.00–18.00, Tues–21.00, daily.*

### Théâtre National de Chaillot
Situated beneath the forecourt of the Palais de Chaillot opposite the Eiffel Tower, the Théâtre National de Chaillot has three auditoriums: the Salle Jean Vilar with some 1,250 seats, the Salle Gémier with 420 seats, and a small studio seating 80. Plays principally from the 19th and 20th centuries are performed here, as well as dance.
*1 place du Trocadéro, 75116,*
*Tel 53 65 30 04,*
*www.theatre-chaillot.fr*

## SPORT, GAMES, FUN

### Cinéaqua
A large aquarium, which includes the biggest tank in France. Around 500 different species of fish from a variety of water-based environments from all over the world are displayed in more than 43 tanks. There are also cinema screens showing films about the sea and envi-

**204 Paris**

# FAUBOURG SAINT-GERMAIN

**Drama and dance both feature on the playlist at the Théâtre National de Chaillot.**

ronmental issues, plus games around the subject for young visitors. A large cinema completes the facilities on offer.
*5 avenue Albert de Mun, 75016, Tel 40 69 23 23, www.cineaqua.com, 10.00–20.00, daily.*

## Les Marionnettes du Champs-de-Mars

A wonderful puppet show for children and a great place to go to keep them occupied on rainy days. Adults can enjoy a drink or eat crêpes during the performance, whilst keeping an eye on their offspring.
*67 rue Croix Nivert, 75007, Tel 01 48 56 01 44. Wed, Sat, Sun, 15.15 and 16.15.*

# SHOPPING

## Alain Mikli

Alain Mikli, optician and spectacle frame designer, has a special philosophy when it comes to his profession: he believes glasses are not only for seeing, but also to be seen in, and that glasses reveal a lot about who you are, as they express your personality. There is a wide range of frames available at Mikli, and some of them are really quite extravagant – they are admittedly also rather expensive –, but when it comes to style, function is never forgotten.
*74 rue des Saints-Pères, 75007, Tel 45 49 40 00, www.mikli.fr, Mon–Sat 10.00–19.00.*

## Le Bon Marché

Another of the city's famous department stores. People don't just come here to shop but to witness a part of history. With the foundation of Bon Marché in 1848, a completely new type of shopping experience was created – the department store. Émile Zola left a literary memorial to the store in his novel *Au Bonheur des Dames*, which deals with the birth of modern retailing. Over the last 20 years, the new owners have transformed Le Bon Marché into a luxury store, which also holds occasional art exhibitions.
*24 rue de Sèvres, 75007, Tel 44 39 80 00, www.lebonmarche.fr, Mon–Wed, Fri 9.30–19.00, Sat 9.30–20.00, Thurs 9.30–21.00.*

## Marie-Anne Cantin Fromagerie

Marie-Anne Cantin pretty much grew up in a cheese shop. In 1982, she followed in the footsteps of her father and opened her own cheese store. Due to the range and quality of her products, she suppliesthe Élysée Palace as well as many restaurants. In France, a country in which –

Paris 205

# COMPACT PARIS

*In the plain, almost canteen-like dining room at the Tokyo Eat you can enjoy top-quality food.*

as de Gaulle said – there is a different cheese for each day of the year, a visit to this fromagerie is a definite must for cheese lovers.
*12 rue du Champ-de-Mars, 75007, Tel 45 50 43 94, www.cantin.fr, Mon 14.00–19.30, Tues–Fri 8.30 to 19.30, Sat 8.30–13.00.*

### Ryst Dupeyron
Connoisseurs of both good Bordeaux wines and Armagnac brandies will be in heaven at Ryst Dupeyron. The selection here is vast. It also sells superb wines from the Rhône, Loire, and Burgundy regions of France, as well as a good selection of whisky, port, and champagne. And if you need a corkscrew or a carafe for decanting wines, both are also available here.
*79 rue du Bac, 75007, Tel 45 48 80 93, www.dupeyron.com, Mon 12.30–19.30, Tues–Sat 10.30–19.30.*

## EATING AND DRINKING

### Le Jules Verne
A top restaurant, serving outstanding international dishes in a top location. The view from this unique restaurant at 125 m (410 ft) height, is simply fabulous, particularly in the evening, when the lights of the city glitter below. Top chef Alain Ducasse has run the kitchens since 2007.
*Second platform of the Eiffel Tower; Tel 45 55 61 44, www.restaurants-toureiffel.com, 12.15–13.30, 18.30–21.30, daily.*

### Tokyo Eat
Chef Thierry Bassard has no problem with guests keeping an eye on him, which is just as well as you can see into the kitchens of the restaurant from the dining room. The name does not reflect the range of the menu; some Japanese meals are served, but also dishes such as risotto and lasagna. It is decorated with numerous works of art, so your visit to the museum extends into the restaurant.
*Palais de Tokyo, 13 avenue du Président Wilson, 75016, Tel 47 20 00 29, www.tokoyeat.com, 12.00–23.30, daily.*

### Zebra Square
This modern restaurant offers cuisine with many different influences from breakfast and lunch through to the evening meal. Traditional dishes are served here, as well as innovative Mediterranean foods, all with a focus on seafood and fresh fish. The weekend brunch is popular with types from the nearby Maison de la Radio.

# FAUBOURG SAINT-GERMAIN

Zebra Square: Mediterranean and Middle Eastern dishes in exotic surroundings.

*3 place Clément Ader, 75016, Tel 44 14 91 91, www.zebrasquare.com, Sun–Wed 8.00–12.00, Thurs–Sat 8.00–1.00.*

## ACCOMMODATION

### Amélie
Each of the rooms in this charming little hotel, located midway between the Eiffel Tower and the Hôtel des Invalides, is decorated in a different shade. Although in a quiet location, a whole range of attractions can be reached easily on foot.
*5 rue Amélie, 75007, Tel 45 51 74 75, www.hotelamelie-paris.com*

### Hôtel Eiffel Rive Gauche
This hotel attempts to bring a little of the warmth and vibrancy of southern France to Paris with its décor and Mediterranean plants in the entrance and lobby. There are 29 rooms, nine of which – the most coveted – have a view of the Eiffel Tower.
*6 rue du Gros-Caillou, 75007, Tel 45 51 24 56, www.hotel-eiffel.com*

### Hôtel la Bourdonnais
The 56 spacious rooms are cozily furnished and decorated in lively shades, with antiques and Persian carpets providing a touch of sophistication. The breakfast room is particularly pretty and the small conservatory garden green and lush.
*111–113 avenue de la Bourdonnais, Tel 47 05 45 42, www.hotellabourdonnais.com*

## NIGHTLIFE

### La Pagode
Built at the turn of the 20th century as a ballroom, La Pagode was converted into a cinema in the 1930s. In the 1970s, however, it faced closure, and was only saved with the efforts of such prominent movie people as film director, Louis Malle. Today it shows arthouse films, and after the performance filmgoers can discuss the merits of the cinematography.
*57 bis rue de Babylone, 75007, Tel 45 55 48 48.*

### L'Étoile
An exclusive mix of restaurant, bar, and club is frequented by the very rich: actors, fashion designers, and major industrialists. The up-scale restaurant will please the most exacting gourmets. The music varies, but disco, house, and electro are all very popular.
*12 rue de Presbourg, 75016, Tel 45 00 78 70, Restaurant: Mon–Sat 12.00–14.00, 20.00–21.00, 23.00–1.00, Sat only 20.00–21.00, 23.00–1.00; Disco: Tues–Sat from 23.00.*

# COMPACT PARIS

The Musée de Montmartre gives a nostalgic retrospective of the glory years in the artists' district.

## MUSEUMS, MUSIC, DRAMA

### L'Élysée Montmartre
The stars of the music scene perform in this ornate 19th-century building. Fashion shows are also held here, and the famous "Bal de l'Élysée" takes place on alternate Saturdays, with dancing through the night.
*72 boulevard Rochechouart, 75018, Tel 42 57 87 19.*

### Le Funambule de Montmartre
This small playhouse has been staging performances for young and old alike for almost 20 years. Plus concerts and themed weeks of festivities.
*53 rue des Saules, 75018, Tel 42 23 88 83, www.funambule-montmartre.com*

### Musée de l'Éventail
Established in 1993, this is the only museum in France devoted to fans. It is housed in the former showrooms of fan manufacturer Lepault & Deberghe dating from 1893. Fans from the 18th to 20th century are on display.
*2 boulevard de Strasbourg, 75010, Tel 42 08 90 20, www.annehoguet.fr/musee.htm, Mon–Wed 14.00–18.00.*

### Musée de Montmartre
This museum explores the rich cultural history of Montmartre – from its early days before the artists and bohemians arrived until today. There is detailed information from the heyday of Montmartre with its many studios and spectacular artists' festivals, but the darker chapters of the area, such as the time of the Paris Commune, are not left out.
*12 rue Cortot, 75018, Tel 49 25 89 37, www.museedemontmartre.fr, Tues–Sun 11.00–18.00.*

### Musée Édith Piaf
This small two-room museum dedicated to the inimitable French singer was set up by her fans. The museum contains mementoes of Piaf, the "sparrow of Paris", including her typical black dresses and her tiny shoes.
*5 rue Crespin-du-Gast, 75011, Tel 43 55 53 72, Mon–Thurs 13.00–18.00, by appointment only.*

### Théâtre de la Porte Saint-Martin
With 1,050 seats, this theater is one of the largest in Paris. The original building was constructed in 1781 as an opera house, and it became a theater in 1831. The current building was erected in record time in 1873 after a fire. In addition to the classics of French drama, musicals and comedies are also staged, often with actors from the world of cinema.

# FURTHER AFIELD

*Musée Édith Piaf: a homage to the "sparrow of Paris".*

18 boulevard Saint-Martin,
75010, Tel 42 08 00 32,
www.portestmartin.com

## FESTIVALS AND EVENTS

### Fête des Vendanges
Amazing although it may seem Paris has its own small vineyard, located on the hillside of Montmartre between Rue Saint-Vincent and Rue des Saules. Every year, the 18th arrondissement stages a festival for the grape harvest (vendange). There are also stalls selling food and drink.
*Montmartre, the weekend between 1 and 10 Oct.*

### French Open
The French Open takes place every year in the Roland Garros stadium. The Grand Slam tournament is one of the most prestigious fixtures on the international tennis calendar and the only one of importance to be played on clay. The stadium is on the edge of the Bois de Boulogne.
*Stade Roland Garros,
2 avenue Gordon-Bennett,
75016, Tel 47 43 48 00,
www.rolandgarros.com,
End of May/beginning of June.*

### Jazz à la Villette
The international jazz elite meets every year in the Parc de la Villette. Concerts are held at various venues throughout the park (the Cité de la Musique, the Grande Halle de la Villette, Théâtre Paris-Villette) and at venues outside the park.
*Parc de la Villette,
End of Aug/beginning Sept.*

## SPORT, GAMES, FUN

### Musée en Herbe
An art museum for children in the Bois de Boulogne. Its aim is to help children become more familiar with art and to make them feel at ease with it by means of games and activities, as well as exhibitions.
*Jardin d'Acclimatation,
Bois de Boulogne, 75016,
Tel 40 67 97 66,
www.musee-en-herbe.com,
10.00–18.00, daily.*

### Keep-fit trail in the Bois de Boulogne
In addition to the miles of footpaths, cycle routes, and bridle path networks, there is also a keep-fit jogging trail in the Bois de Boulogne, which is 2.5 km (1.5 miles) in length. At 19 stops along the route, gym equipment is provided so that you can pause to do some additional crosstraining exercises. A note of caution: it is not advisable to remain in the Bois de Boulogne after dark.
*Starting point: Carrefour des 5 Routes, about half-way along avenue de Saint-Cloud.*

**Paris** 209

# COMPACT PARIS

**The brightly lit façade of the Tati department store.**

## SHOPPING

### Christophe Delcourt
This shop specializes in lamps and furniture of modern, elegant, clean designs, in wood and black steel.
*39 rue Lucien Sampaix, 75010, Tel 42 71 34 84,
www.christophedelcourt.com
Mon–Fri 9.00–12.00, 13.00–18.00.*

### Tati
If you're looking for bargains in Paris, head for a branch of the cut-price Tati department-store chain.
*4 boulevard de Rochechouart, 75018, Tel 55 59 52 50,
www.tati.fr,
Mon–Sat 10.00–19.00.*

## EATING AND DRNKING

### Au Boeuf Couronné
Dating back to 1865, this restaurant has retained many original fittings from the belle époque. As the name hints, beef dishes are the focus here.
*188 avenue Jean Jaurès, 75019, Tel 42 39 44 44,
12.00–15.00, 19.00–24.00, daily.*

### Globe Trotter Café
In the middle of La Défense, this café transports you to far warmer climes. Palms provide a tropical ambience while the menu hails from France's overseas colonies.
*15 place de la Défense, 92800 La Défense, Tel 55 91 96 96,
Mon–Fri 12.00–14.30.*

### Hôtel du Nord
The hotel boasts an extensive wine list to accompany its traditional dishes. A must for fans of French cinema, who will be taken back to the 1938 French classic L'Hôtel du Nord.
*102 quai de Jemmapes, 75010, Tel 40 40 78 78,
www.hoteldunord.org,
Café: 9.00–1.30, daily
Restaurant: 12.00–15.00, 20.00–24.00, daily.*

### Le Potager du Père Thierry
If you're in the mood for tasty and original bistro cuisine just a short distance from bustling Montmartre, then this is the place for you. Reservation is recommended.
*16 rue Trois Frères, 75018, Tel 53 28 26 20,
19.00–24.00, daily,
Fri–Sun 12.00–14.00.*

### Le Poulbot
Traditional Montmartre atmosphere in this restaurant named after Francisque Poulbot, the French artist famed for drawings of Montmartre street urchins in the 1900s.
*3 rue Poulbot, 75018, Tel 42 23 32 07,
www.lepoulbot.fr,
from 11.00, daily.*

# FURTHER AFIELD

The legendary Moulin Rouge is an institution, and Paris is unimaginable without it.

### Le Pré Catelan
Delicious three-star Michelin haute cuisine, served by chef Frédéric Anton in a pavilion dating from Napoleon III.
*Route de Suresnes,*
*Bois de Boulogne, 75016,*
*Tel 44 14 41 14,*
*www.precatelanparis.com,*
*Tues–Sat 12.00–14.00, 19.30–22.30.*

## ACCOMMODATION

### Comfort Hôtel Place du Tertre
A charming small hotel with 46 small but cozy rooms in the heart of Montmartre, not far from all the main sights.
*16 rue Tholozé, 75018,*
*Tel 42 55 05 06,*
*www.comfort-placedutertre.com*

### Ermitage Hôtel
Rooms – there are 12 in all – in country-house style at reasonable rates. The breakfast room is small, but breakfast is also served in the rooms or in the romantic courtyard in fine weather.
*24 rue Lamarck, 75018,*
*Tel 42 64 79 22,*
*www.ermitagesacrecoeur.fr*

### Murano Urban Resort
A sleek five-star hotel with a high-tech modern décor – mood lighting in different hues which can be controlled at the flick of a switch; chrome and slate bathrooms, and guests use a fingerprint not keys to access their rooms.
*13 boulevard du Temple,*
*75010, Tel 42 71 20 00,*
*www.muranoresort.com*

### Terrass Hôtel
A four-star hotel with the added attraction of a rooftop terrace restaurant. Le Diapason serves traditional dishes with a Mediterranean twist, all with a fine view of the city.
*12–14 rue Joseph Maistre,*
*75018, Tel 46 06 72 85,*
*www.terrass-hotel.com*

## NIGHTLIFE

### Au Lapin Agile
A famous cabaret venue for the classic French chanson. The sign with the rabbit (lapin) jumping out of a hat has hung here since 1880.
*22 rue des Saules, 75018,*
*Tel 46 06 85 87,*
*www.aulapinagile.com,*
*Tues–Sun 21.00–2.00.*

### Moulin Rouge
The famous Moulin Rouge is named after the model of a red windmill on its roof. It was founded in 1889 and is still entertaining visitors today with its lavish revues.
*Bal du Moulin Rouge,*
*82 boulevard de Clichy,*
*75018, Tel 53 09 82 82,*
*www.moulinrouge.fr*

Paris 211

# COMPACT PARIS

At the Musée des Carrosses in Versailles you can visit the splendid carriages of the French kings and queens.

MUSEUMS, MUSIC, DRAMA

### Musée d'Art et d'Histoire, Saint-Denis
This museum dedicated to art and history has found a stylish home in a former Carmelite convent. One of the focuses of the exhibits is sacred art; but several rooms are also devoted to the uprising against the Paris Commune in 1871. Three artists deserve attention – the artist and painter Honoré Daumier, the painter and designer Francis Jourdain, and the poet Paul Eluard.
*22 bis rue Gabriel Péri, 93200 Saint-Denis, Tel 42 43 05 10, www.musee-saint-denis.fr Mon, Wed, Fri 10.00–17.30, Thurs 10.00–20.00, Sat, Sun 14.00–18.30.*

### Musée des Carrosses, Versailles
This carriage museum is found in a former stable block of the chateau at Versailles. A wide range of carriages and coaches are on display, some of which are highly ornate, including those commissioned for the wedding of Napoleon Bonparte to Marie-Louise, his second wife, the carriage that took French King Charles X to his coronation, and the hearse of Louis XVIII. In addition, there are six royal sleighs and four sedan chairs dating from the 18th and 19th centuries – it all reminds you that the kings' horses were better cared for than some of their subjects.
*1 avenue Rockefeller, 78000 Versailles, Tel 30 83 77 88, www.yvelines.fr/culturel/ musees/40_musée.htm*

### Théâtre du Soleil, Vincennes
A former munitions factory – La Cartoucherie – is now home to this arts complex. Ariane Mnouchkine is the resident director at the Théâtre du Soleil, the best known of the venues here. Film and theatrical director Mnouchkine founded the playhouse in 1964 and has enjoyed great international success since then. She is always willing to explore something new, often by incorporating theatrical forms from other countries in her work. Whatever pieces are being staged, classic or modern, performances at the Cartoucherie are always interesting.
*Cartoucherie, route du Champ de Manœuvre, 75012 Paris, Tel 43 74 87 63, www.theatre-du-soleil.fr*

SPORT, GAMES, FUN

### Parc Zoologique de Paris, Vincennes
Part of the Muséum national de l'Histoire naturelle, the Paris zoo was established in the Bois de Vincennes in 1934. The

# BEYOND PARIS

Giraffes at the Parc Zoologique de Paris in Vincennes.

65-m (213-foot) high Grand Rocher, a man-made rock, is home to mountain animals, such as sure-footed goats. Visitors can also climb the rock if they wish, allowing them access to the animals.
*53 avenue de Saint Maurice, 75012 Paris, Tel 44 75 20 00, www.mnhn.fr, Mon–Sat 9.00–18.00, Sun 9.00–18.30.*

**Studio Tram Tour, Disneyland**
This tour starts as a peaceful tram ride, but as soon as you enter "Catastrophe Canyon" the trip suddenly gets a little less comfortable as you are confronted with the full force of nature – fire, water, an earthquake – the fantastic special effects all take the unsuspecting visitor by surprise on this adrenaline-filled ride.
*Disneyland Resort Paris, Marne-la-Vallée, Tel 08 25 30 60 30, www.disneylandparis.com, 10.00–23.00, daily.*

## SHOPPING

**Librairie des Enfants, Versailles**
This children's bookstore is a paradise for all tiny bookworms – there are 10,000 books on sale for the smallest of readers in an area of 200 sq m (239 sq yds). Various events are also held with the aim of introducing children to the world of reading and books.
*24 rue du Vieux-Versailles, 78000 Versailles, Tel 39 50 05 09, http://pagesperso-orange.fr/librairie.des.enfants*

**Potager du Roi, Versailles**
Even when the king of France was still the ruler of all he surveyed, including this royal fruit and vegetable garden, the excess produce of the garden was given away to the people of Versailles. Today, the fruits from the garden are sold along with delicious homemade jams, juices, and sweets.
*10 rue du Maréchal Joffre, 78000 Versailles, www.potager-du-roi.fr, April–mid-Dec, Tues–Sun 10.00–18.00.*

## EATING AND DRINKING

**La Marée de Versailles**
There's a rather Greek look to the blue-painted wooden façade of this restaurant in Versailles, which serves outstanding fish and seafood dishes. You can also eat at outside if the weather allows. Reservations can be made online.
*22 rue au Pain, 78000 Versailles, Tel 30 21 73 73, www.restaurantlamaree.com, Tues–Sat 12.00–14.00, 19.15–22.00.*

Paris 213

# COMPACT PARIS

*The impressive façade of the Hôtel Aigle Noir Fontainebleau.*

## La Brasserie de la Malmaison

The brasserie is housed in the building that was one of the two former pavilions marking the entrance to the chateau of Malmaison's park. Today, the wooden panels lining the dining room walls create a warm and pleasant homely atmosphere in which traditional dishes from the French provinces are served. The kitchen is skilled at producing specialty dishes from the Alsace, such as the sauerkraut and meat dish known as "choucroute garni" or the lovely, savoury tarte flambée, known as "flammekueche".
*193 avenue Napoléon Bonaparte, 92500 Rueil-Malmaison, Tel 47 51 82 83, www.brasseriemalmaison.com*

## L'Archipel, Vincennes

This is the place to try if you want to discover a relatively unknown culinary style. The chef Andreza Varis hails from the Cape Verde Islands, where he learned his craft. As you might expect, fish and seafood play a large part in his island cuisine, often served in combinations that are both interesting and unusual to European tastes. The restaurant also runs on Cape Verde time, which is a little more relaxed – on the restaurant's website homepage, opening times are simply described as "lunchtimes" and "evenings".
*35 bis rue de Montreuil, 94300 Vincennes, Tel 41 93 06 17, Mon–Sat lunchtimes, Thurs, Fri evenings.*

## Le Petit Bofinger

Located in the immediate vicinity of the chateau de Vincennes, this restaurant serves traditional French dishes of a very high quality.
*2 avenue de Paris, 94300 Vincennes, Tel 01 43 28 25 76.*

## ACCOMMODATION

### Hôtel Aigle Noir, Fontainebleau

This stylish hotel is located in the former residence of an aristocratic family, dating from the 17th century. All the rooms and suites are individually furnished in Empire style and the hotel is equipped with modern facilities, including a bar and fitness room.
*27 place Napoléon Bonaparte, 77300 Fontainebleau, Tel 60 74 60 00, www.hotelaiglenoir.com*

### Hôtel des Arts, Rueil Malmaison

Situated in a beautifully calm location in an historic district, the pastel shades of the rooms in this modern hotel also

# BEYOND PARIS

Guests can expect grand surroundings at the Hotel Trianon Palace in Versailles.

radiate a pleasant air of peace. In fine, warm weather, you can enjoy breakfast in the hotel's quiet inner patio and garden.
*3 boulevard du Maréchal Joffre, 92500 Rueil Malmaison, Tel 47 52 15 00, www.hoteldesartsrueil.fr*

### Hôtel du Château, Vincennes
This 19-room hotel is located close to the RER station and the château at Vincennes. It has recently been renovated. The arms and swords that are now displayed in the hotel lobby, and the interior design and décor, are a reminder – albeit a slightly labored effort – that heroic knights once inhabited the nearby medieval chateau and hunting lodge. There is an excellent view of the chateau from some of the bedrooms.
*1 rue Robert Giraudineau, 94300 Vincennes, Tel 48 08 67 40, http://www.hotel-chateau-vincennes.federal-hotel.com/*

### Hôtel Napoléon, Fontainebleau
The generously proportioned, modern rooms and public spaces of this hotel surround an immaculate inner court yard, filled with lush greenery. As for the old building itself, Napoleon himself might have once looked out onto it when he was in residence in the nearby chateau.
*9 rue Grande, 77300 Fontainebleau, Tel 60 39 50 50, www.hotel-napoleon-fontainebleau.com*

### La Résidence du Berry, Versailles
This sophisticated hotel, with its 38 individual and modern rooms, is just a few minutes on foot from the chateau at Versailles. The old wine cellar vaults are filled with numerous bottles of vintage wine, which is served at the hotel bar. It also has a billiards table.
*14 rue d'Anjou, 78000 Versailles, Tel 39 49 07 07, www.hotel-berry.com*

### Trianon Palace, Versailles
This stylish luxury four-star hotel is located in a magnificent park and woodlands, only a few miles from the chateau of Versailles. Guests may expect royal-style luxury and a matching ambience. It also has a spa. The hotel restaurant boasts a total of three Michelin stars – British TV star, chef Gordon Ramsay provides the very best of gastronomic pleasures. in the very ornate dining rooms.
*1 Boulevard de la Reine, 78000 Versailles, Tel 30 84 50 00, www.trianonpalace.com*

In the middle of the Cour Napoléon, the Louvre's inner courtyard, the glass pyramid offers excellent views of the museum's three wings; seen here is the Aile Richelieu wing.

# MAJOR MUSEUMS

Think of a subject and Paris will probably have a museum dedicated to it – whether its European art through the centuries, the art of other continents, technology, natural history, or any other specialist interest such as fashion or musical instruments – visitors with a specific interest, certainly won't be disappointed. Ranging from enormous museums, to small, intimate exhibits in the former homes of artists – all have their own attraction. But the flagship of the Parisian museums has to be the Louvre, one of the largest and most important museums in the world housing equally famous works of art.

# MAJOR MUSEUMS

The Louvre has been a museum since 1793, but it was transformed during the last decades of the 20th century. The Glass Pyramid designed by architect I.M. Pei now forms the entrance to the museum. The rooms have been markedly enlarged; the Ministry of Finance, which used to be housed in the north wing, was moved to a new building in Berc. This made room for exhibits that until then were consigned to the stock rooms. Since 1200, successive French monarchs, from Philippe II onwards, have built and rebuilt the Louvre, for centuries their main palace. Pierre Lescot designed the Cour Carrée, one of the most splendid parts of the building for François I. King Henri IV commissioned the Grande Galerie on the banks of the Seine in order to create a harmonious link between the Louvre and the Tuileries, a decisive change in the appearance of the palace.

The exhibits of the Louvre are divided into several separate collections: Egyptian antiquities, oriental antiquities, Islamic art, Greek, Etruscan, and Roman antiquities, arts and crafts, sculpture, paintings, and drawings. Each of these collections includes great masterpieces of the very finest quality; here we shall only highlight some of the departments whose collections are unrivaled in the world.

## EGYPTIAN ANTIQUITIES

Some of the statuettes of the Old Kingdom are fascinatingly realistic, including the Seated Scribe (c. 2500 BC) and the double portrait of the Inspector of Scribes Raherka and his Wife (c. 2350 BC). There are also some interesting works dating from the New Kingdom, such as the well-preserved bas-relief of the goddess of heaven Hathor, worshipped as a cow-deity, receiving King Sethos I (c. 1200 BC), or the head of a colossal statue of pharoah Amenophis III (c. 1380 BC), who had the Temple of Amun built in Luxor, among others. There are also some beautiful portraits painted on wood from the Roman period in Egypt on display.

## GREEK, ETRUSCAN, AND ROMAN ANTIQUITIES

Two of the most famous sculptures in the museum are contained in this collection: the remarkable Winged Victory of Samothrace and the Venus de Milo. The statue of Nike, the Greek goddess of victory, was sculpted in around 190 BC to commemorate the Greek victory in a sea battle against the Syrians. It is sculpted as though the winged goddess has just landed; her wings are still outspread, she has one foot forward, and the wind catches the folds of her robe. Although the statue is sadly missing its head, it is easy to imagine the powerful impression she made on people when she was erected in her original site in the port of the island of Samothrace in the Aegean Sea. Sculpted in about 100 BC, the statue of Venus de Milo, who, as a Greek, should in reality be named Aphrodite, is much more statuesque than the Winged Victory, but the timeless beauty of her face and figure have fascinated people over the centuries. The Lady from Auxerre (c. 630 BC), a female stauette from the Greek Archaicum and about 75 cm (29 in) tall, seems no less important. Without doubt, one of the most outstanding testimonies of Etruscan art, is the sarco-

# LOUVRE

Left: The glass pyramid, just under 22 m (72 ft) high, has served as the main entrance to the Louvre since 1989. From the lower floor escalators and corridors lead to all the museum's wings. Below: Egyptian figures and a wooden container depicting scenes from the Egyptian Book of the Dead (1080–714 BC).

# MAJOR MUSEUMS

## MONA LISA

The most reproduced and parodied painting in art history, your first sight of Leonardo da Vinci's masterpiece may come as a shock – it is tiny in comparison with many great paintings, measuring just 77 x 53 cm (30 x 20 inches). It is said to depict Lisa del Giocondo, wife of a Florentine merchant. Leonardo began the painting during a stay in Florence in around 1502 or 1503, and he never went anywhere without it. Thus it arrived in France in 1516, when he was invited to work at Amboise by François I. The king bought the painting and kept it at Fontainebleau, then at Versailles, and

---

phagus of a couple at rest (late 6th century BC), formed from terracotta, which had been unearthed in the Etruscan necropolis of Cerveteri.

In addition to these two major works, there are many other statues, red- and black-figured pottery, works of art, and elaborately decorated household utensils such as ancient mirrors and oil lamps that make fascinating viewing.

## PAINTINGS

The painting collection is dominated by French and Italian masterpieces, but some excellent works from the Netherlands, Flanders, Spain, England, and Germany are also represented. Just a few outstanding examples from each country include Jan Vermeer's *The Lacemaker*, Jan van Eyck's *The Virgin of Chancellor Rolin*, Francisco de Goya's *The Countess of Carpio*, Thomas Gainsborough's *The Artist and his Wife*, and Hans Holbein's *Erasmus of Rotterdam*.

The collection of Italian paintings naturally includes the most famous painting in the Louvre, if not the world, the *Mona Lisa* (see panel, above), but it would be a mistake to overlook the richness of other outstanding Italian paintings from different eras because of Leonardo's masterpiece.

Leonardo da Vinci himself is also represented in other works (such as *Anna Selbdritt*), as are Giotto (*St Francis of Assisi Receiving the Stigmata*), Veronese (including *The Wedding at Cana*), Raphael (including *Baldassare Castiglione*), Titian, Tintoretto, Pisanello, Caravaggio, Canaletto, and many others with some of their very best works. The French painting collection also provides an interesting and rather detailed overview of its development; the best-known works include Jean-Antoine Watteau's *Gilles*, Jacques-Louis David's *The Oath of the Horatii*, Théodore Géricault's *The Raft of the Medusa*, Jean-Dominique-Auguste Ingres' *La Grande Odalisque*, Eugène Delacroix's *Liberty Leading the People*, as well as Jean-Baptiste Camille Corot's *Chartres Cathedral*.

A few of the most famous portraits of French kings have also found a home at the Musée du Louvre including Jean Fouquet's *Charles V* (1403–1461); Jean Clouet's *Portrait of Francis I* (1494-1547); and Hyacinthe Rigaud's *Louis XIV* (1638– 1715).

However, many visitors will find other paintings to which they are drawn among works that are less well known, but are still worthy of their place in this world-famous Museum.

# LOUVRE

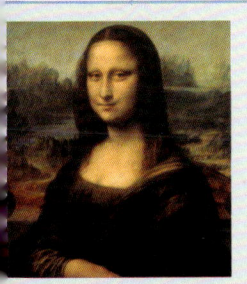

it finally made its way to the Louvre. In 1911, it was stolen by Italian Vincenzo Peruggia, who wanted to repatriate it to Italy. The painting was lost for more than two years; it was rediscovered when Peruggia tried to sell it. Since an acid attack in 1956, Mona Lisa has smiled from behind bulletproof glass. Art critics believe that the painting suffers from the change in lighting.

**Leonardo da Vinci's *Mona Lisa*, also known under the title *La Gioconda*. Her mysterious smile has puzzled art lovers and art for centuries.**

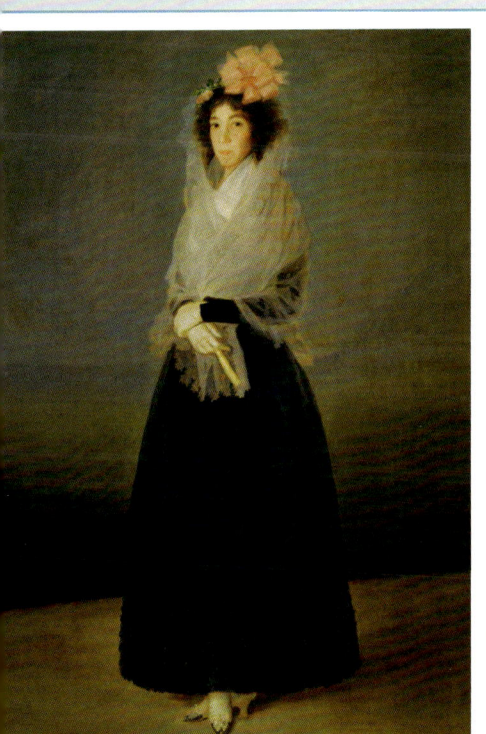

## OTHER COLLECTIONS

One of the star attractions among the oriental antiquities is the stele of the Babylonian king Hammurabi, the Codex Hammurabi, one of the earliest collections of written laws. Michelangelo's *Dying Slave* is considered a masterpiece of sculpture. Among the drawings deserving attention is a delicate *Virgin and Child* by the German artist Stefan Lochner and the *Portrait of Isabella d'Este* by Leonardo da Vinci.

*Musée du Louvre, 34–36 quai du Louvre, Tel 40 20 58 24, www.louvre.fr, Wed–Mon 9.00–18.00, (Wed and Thurs to 22.00), Métro Palais Royal/ Musée du Louvre.*

*The Countess of Carpio, died 1795*, oil on canvas, by Francisco de Goya, 1794.

Paris 221

# MAJOR MUSEUMS

The late-Gothic building has been a museum since 1843, but its roots extend back into antiquity; the remains of Roman thermal baths found there date from around 200. Inside the building you can now find an outstanding collection of art from the Middle Ages. Along with the Hôtel de Sens, the Hôtel de Cluny – home to the Musée National du Moyen Age (National Museum of the Middle Ages) – is one of the oldest preserved town houses in Paris. The Abbey of Cluny acquired the land at the start of the 14th century; the Abbot Jacques d'Amboise later took it over as his residence, re-building in a flamboyant late-Gothic style between 1485 and 1510. From 1600, the palace was an occasional residence for the Papal Legate and from 1747 the complex's tower was used as an observatory. The thermal baths were unearthed on the orders of Louis XVIII in 1819.

The museum actually consists of two quite different buildings – the Hôtel de Cluny, which houses the collections of medieval art assembled by the passionate collector and archaeologist Alexandre du Sommerard (1779–1842), and the remains of the Roman thermal baths.

## MEDIEVAL ART

If you wish to experience medieval art in all its various forms, you are at the right place. Exquisite examples of all kinds of medieval art, from Romanesque to Gothic, are exhibited in a perfect setting in the Hôtel de Cluny. Romanesque art is represented in a collection of sculptures, frescoes, precious illuminated manuscripts, and stained-glass windows from all over Europe – from Catalonia and Sicily in the south, to Saxony in the east, and Britain in the north. You can see carved capitals from the most important Parisian abbeys, including those of Sainte-Geneviève, Saint-Germain-des-Prés, and Saint-Denis, as well as beautiful stained-glass windows from Saint-Denis. The museum also boasts significant examples of gold and ivory carvings. Some of the best-known pieces come from Toledo in Spain, including the two Visigoth votive crowns bearing the names of kings Suinthila and Rekkeswinth. Another masterpiece is the altar frontal from the minster in Basel, commissioned by King Henri II at the start of the 11th century. He is depicted at Christ's feet. Other fine examples of the work of goldsmiths are the enamel works from Limoges, while the ivory carvings on display stand comparison with those in the Louvre and provide an overview of life from Late Antiquity to the late Middle Ages. Examples of secular pieces (such as mirrors, combs, and caskets) are displayed alongside sacred art (altarpieces and crosses). Among the tapestries on display, by far the most significant ones belong to the series known as *The Lady and the Unicorn* (see page 10).

The many other works on show provide a solid overview of medieval art – the different techniques used and the range of subject matter, from the early to late Middle Ages, coming from Iran, Egypt, and Byzantium, to Italy, Spain, England, Flanders, and, of course, France.

Also on show from the Parisian abbeys are wall hangings that decorated the walls of the oratories. Dating from the 15th century, they depict some 2 scenes from the life of St Stephen and were produced i

# MUSÉE NATIONAL DU MOYEN ÂGE – MUSÉE DE CLUNY

Left: The courtyard of the Hôtel de Cluny. The complex also comprises imaginatively laid out gardens, with culinary and healing herbs growing in the Jardin Médiéval.

Below: Musée de Cluny, *Le Sacre de Louis XII* (The Anointment of Louis XII), oil on canvas, 1502.

# MAJOR MUSEUMS

## THE LADY AND THE UNICORN

This series of six tapestries, produced in Flanders toward the end of the 15th century, eventually found their way via a circuitous route to the château at Boussac in France, where they were discovered in the 19th century by Prosper Mérimée, author and historian, and official chief inspector of historic monuments. They were incorporated into the Musée de Cluny's collections in 1882. Five of the six tapestries represent the five senses, but the sixth is something of a mystery. It bears the words a mon seul désir (to my only desire) on the canopy in front of which the lady stands flanked by a li-

the tapestry workshop at Auxerre. There are also examples of fabrics from that time, including silks from Byzantium that were sought-after by the Carolingians and later the Italian silks in the 15th century. While the Western world made only plain fabrics for everyday use, the finest fabrics had to be imported from the Orient until well into the Middle Ages. There are many examples of textiles used in the church, such as altar cloths, liturgical garments, and covers for reliquaries. Other star attractions in the museum's collection are the illuminated manuscripts, presented along with frescoes, paintings, and stained-glass windows as arts de la couleur (the art of color). Visitors can also gain a fascinating insight into the everyday life of people in the Middle Ages with displays of ordinary objects. As well as chests and caskets, pewter and ceramic tableware, shoes, combs, articles of clothing, there are many personal items on display, as well as objects that were taken on pilgrimages (to Santiago de Compostela, Rome, etc.).

## THE KINGS OF NOTRE-DAME

For about three decades, the sculpture collection has owned the statues of the kings taken from the Cathedral of Notre-Dame. It wasn't just the living king Louis XVI who lost his head – in 1793 the Revolutionaries removed the heads from the statues of the biblical kings, believing them to be former French rulers. Long presumed lost, their effigies were eventually replaced on Notre-Dame with copies. But in 1977, during building work some 2 km (2,187 yards) from the cathedral, 21 of the heads were rediscovered. They now form one of the showpieces of the collection of the Musée National du Moyen Age.

## THE ROMAN THERMAL BATHS

The Roman thermal baths, located here not far from the Cardo and Decumanus maximus – as today's boulevards Saint-Germain and Saint-Michel were known at the time – reveal quite a different world from the medieval Paris of the Hôtel de Cluny. Nonetheless, the medieval architects of Hôtel de Cluny integrated the frigidarium (cold bath) of the thermal baths and its vaults into their new building. As the pillars support terminals that look like ships' prows, it is assumed that the nautes – shipowners – of the Roman settlement financed the construction. You can see other

224 Paris

# MUSÉE NATIONAL DU MOYEN ÂGE – MUSÉE DE CLUNY

on and a unicorn. In this sixth tapestry, the lady is placing the necklace, which is worn in the five previous tapestries, in a box. Possible interpretations see her as a symbol of renunciation, virginity, or love.

*The Lady and the Unicorn*, 1495, produced for Jean Le Viste.

remains of the baths in the garden of the museum – the caldarium (a room with a hot plunge bath) and the tepidarium, the warm bathroom. Parts of the gymnasia, or sport halls associated with the baths, also remain.

*Musée National du Moyen Âge,*
*6 place Paul Painlevé,*
*Tel 53 73 78 00,*
*www.musee-moyenage.fr,*
*Wed–Mon 9.15–17.45,*
*Métro Cluny La Sorbonne.*

This Gothic sculpture of Adam, created in 1260, originally adorned, together with a sculpture of Eve, the façade of the southern transept in Notre-Dame. There the figures flanked a scene depicting Jesus at the Last Judgment. The restored figure of Adam can today be seen in a wing of the Musée National du Moyen Âge.

Paris 225

# MAJOR MUSEUMS

Nobody likes paying tax, and inheritance taxes rarely cause a lot of enthusiasm, but in this instance, it has at least been of benefit to the general public. The collection of the Musée National Picasso is primarily based on works donated to the state by the artist's heirs to settle their inheritance tax debt – a large number of works by one of the most pre-eminent masters of the 20th century. Situated in the heart of the Marais, one of the most historic and fashionable districts in Paris, the Hôtel Salé is surrounded by the magnificent 17th- and 18th-century houses of wealthy citizens and the French nobility. Today this beautiful mansion house is home to the Musée National Picasso, which boasts one of the world's largest collections of works by the multitalented master from Málaga in Spain. Unfortunately the museum is closed for extensive renovations, probably until 2012.

## ART AND INHERITANCE TAX

French law allows the heirs of an artist to pay inheritance tax by donating works from the artist's estate. At the same time, the artist's heirs can also stipulate that a museum be established in which to display them. This is precisely what happened when Pablo Picasso, the versatile and talented Spanish artist, died in 1973, leaving no will. His family left to the French state 203 paintings, 158 sculptures, 88 ceramics, 1,500 drawings and collages, and 1,600 etchings, as well as personal documents, with the stipulation that a museum be set up to house them all. Picasso's private collection was initially displayed at the Louvre from 1978, but in 1984 the collection was moved more appropriately to the Musée Picasso. In 1990, when Jacqueline, Picasso's second wife, died, a further 47 paintings, two sculptures, and a series of drawings, ceramic work, and etchings were also donated to the museum to settle inheritance tax debt due on her death.

## FROM THE BLUE TO THE ROSE PERIOD, AND CUBISM

Between his self-portrait of 1901 set against a blue background, and his 1906 self-portrait with a naked torso, his work shows a clear development toward more angular forms, even if Cubism is not fully pronounced in his Rose Period. *Les Demoiselles d'Avignon* represents the actual transition to Cubism. The painting is held in the Museum of Modern Art in New York, although the Musée Picasso has a number of studies for the painting from 1907. Typical Picasso Cubist paintings from the second decade of the 20th century include *L'homme à la guitare* and *L'homme à la mandoline* (both 1911) and still lifes such as *Nature morte à la chaise cannée* (1912) and *Nature morte: Guitare, journal, verre et as de trèfle* (1914).

## THE INTERWAR YEARS

The years between the two World Wars began with Picaso's classical period, and include works that are less well known, and which look at the ideals of beauty in antiquity, such as *Tête de femme*, *Trois femmes à la fontaine* (both 1921) and *La flute de Pan* (1923). However, during the years 1924 and 1925, Picasso also produced two of his best-known images, part of his series of artist and

# MUSÉE NATIONAL PICASSO

Left: The museum, opened in 1985, contains a major part of Picasso's artistic bequest. His entire output is estimated at some 20,000 works of art.
Below: A visitor studies some of the master's works at the Musée National Picasso.
Bottom: Design for a stage curtain, 1920.

# MAJOR MUSEUMS

## THE HÔTEL SALÉ

The Hôtel Salé was built in 1656 to 1659 for aristocrat Pierre Aubert, Seigneur of Fontenay, to plans by architect Jean de Bouiller. The design for the interior was created by Martin Desjardins and the brothers Gaspard and Balthazar Mars. However, Aubert was caught up in the turbulence that surrounded the arrest of the finance minister, Fouquet, and he lost his fortune. In the centuries that followed his elegant palace took on a variety of roles – Venetian embassy, institution for children and young people, central school of arts and crafts, until finally the state purchased the

musician portraits, characterized by great almost photographic realism: *Paul en arlequin* and *Paul en pierrot*. They have been reproduced many thousands of times on different products, ranging from jigsaw puzzles to decorative fridge magnets, and you are bound to have seen a version of them. Pictures inspired by Surrealism include *Le baiser* (1925) and *Le peintre et son modèle* (1926). The Surrealist-inspired work was followed by a series of images of people bathing, such as *Baigneuse* (1928), *Baigneuse ouvrant la cabine* (1928), *Baigneuses sur la plage* (1928) and *Grande baigneuse* (1929). In the 1930s, Pablo Picasso returned to Spain and its great passion for bull-fighting for inspiration; he then produced a series of works on the subject, including, for example, the two versions of *Corrida: la mort du toréro* (both from 1933).

## FROM 1936 TO 1973

In 1936, Picasso met the photographer Dora Maar, who soon became his partner. At the same time she also advanced to become his favorite model in the coming years. Portraits of Dora Maar are regarded as some of the most important works of the period directly before and during the war – three different portraits of her date from 1937 alone. From the postwar years until his death, Picasso mainly lived mostly in the south of France, either directly on the Mediterranean coast (Antibes, Cannes) or in the hinterland of the Côte d'Azur (Vallauris, Vauvenargues). He devoted his time increasingly to ceramics, particularly while in Vallauris, but he still produced paintings of significance during this period, often inspired by his environment: *Fumées à Vallauris* (1951), *La baie de Cannes* (1958), *Paysage* (1972). He also produced his own playful interpretation of Manet's *Déjeuner sur l'herbe* (1961).

## SCULPTURES AND CERAMICS

Along with its paintings, the Musée Picasso also displays many of the artist's sculptures and ceramics.
From early representational formssuchas *Femme assise* (1902), Picasso passed from Cubist representations – such as *Mandoline et clarinette* (1913), mannerist extended figures such as *Femme debou* (several versions, 1930), a very realistic and touching figure *L'homme au mouton* (1943) – to develop highly origina works such as *Femme à la poussette* (1950). Picasso created a large part of his

# MUSÉE NATIONAL PICASSO

building in 1964, when it was declared an historic monument. The building was converted to suit its new use between 1974 and 1984. Sculptor and designer Diego Giacometti carried out work on the interior.

**Inside the Hôtel Salé, home to the Musée National Picasso.**

ceramics during his time at Vallauris, north-east of Cannes They range from dishes, tiles, and plates depicting interesting faces via landscapes, such as in *Fumées à Vallauris* (1951) to street scenes as in *Jeux de pages* (1951). The vases and jugs appear in simple forms and fashioned to represent elaborate designed animal or human figures.

Finally, Picasso also created statues during this time such as *Chouette à tête d'homme* und *Chouette à tête de femme* (1951–1953).

*Musée National Picasso,*
*5 rue de Thorigny,*
*Tel 42 71 25 21,*
*www.musee-picasso.fr,*
*Oct–March Wed–Mon 9.30–17.30, April–Sept Wed–Mon 9.30–18.00.*

**Le Fou (the fool), bronze sculpture, 1905.**

Paris 229

# MAJOR MUSEUMS

The Centre Georges Pompidou is one of the most visited cultural institutions in Europe. As well as enjoying the works of art inside, you can travel from floor to floor via the escalators in transparent tubes mounted on the outside of the building, providing fantastic views over the city. The design for the Centre Pompidou by Renzo Piano and Richard Rogers was pretty controversial right from its opening in 1977. The idea of making the building's infrastructure visible with bright pipes on the exterior was unusual, and led to derisory nicknames such as "the refinery". However, it has long since become one of the famous symbols of the city. Visitors come to the Musée National d'Art Moderne on Levels 4 and 5, to the library (Levels 1 to 3) and to the Galerie d'Exposition on Level 6. The Galerie shows mainly changing exhibitions of contemporary art and retrospectives.

The Musée National d'Art Moderne was opened in the Palais de Tokyo in 1947. In 1977, three decades later, it moved to the newly opened Centre Pompidou, where it currently occupies the fourth and fifth floors and covers an exhibition area of some 14,000 sq m (150,640 sq ft).

Only a small proportion of its total works, which number about 60,000, can be shown at any one time. These have been collected over time through gifts, donations, bequests, being left to the state in lieu of inheritance tax payements, as well as acquisitions by the museum itself.

Contemporary art is housed on the fourth floor, whereas art of the 20th century is shown on the fifth floor. Interesting and spectacular special exhibitions are also held here.

Together, the collections form a history of 20th century art.

## ART OF THE 20TH CENTURY

Art dating from 1905 to 1960 is exhibited on the fifth floor of the building. Rooms are divided according to different criteria and selected artists have a whole room devoted to them and their work.

The first room exhibits works by Georges Rouault, including *Fille au miroir* (1913); but the artist is also represented elsewhere, in Room 29, with later works from the years between 1948 and 1956, including, for example, *Christ au bord du lac* (1949). Another artist whose work can be found in two rooms is Henri Matisse; his earlier paintings include *Le violiniste à la fenêtre* (1918); some of the artist's later works produced in his studio in Vence, Provence, include *Grand intérieur rouge.*, which was purchased by the French government in 1949. Other rooms are allocated to artists of particular styles or groups. Room 26 displays works from the Bauhaus movement, such as a lath chair by Marcel Breuer and a Bauhaus lamp by Wilhelm Wagenfeld. Room 36 shows some of the artists associated with the Galerie Maeght in the 1950s – Pierre Bonnard, *Trouville, la sortie du port*, Alberto Giacometti's *La mère de l'artiste*, and Georges Braque's *L'atelier IX*. There is also a large number of works by Jean Arp, Fernand Léger, Georges Braque, Antoine Pevsner, Alexander Calder, Joan Miró, Alberot Giacometti, Francis Picabia, Pablo Picasso, Robert and Sonia Delaunay, Jean Dubuffet and the American painters, Jackson Pollock, and Mark Rothko. Plenty of space is also given to photographers such as Brassaï and Man Ray.

# CENTRE POMPIDOU – MUSÉE NATIONAL D'ART MODERNE

Left: The pipes' coloration reveals their purpose. Ducts for air are blue, for water, green, and for light, yellow.

Below: Stilleben, Kontrast der Objekte, by Fernand Léger, 1930, Oil on canvas, Musée National d'Art Moderne.

# MAJOR MUSEUMS

## CENTRE POMPIDOU

French President Georges Pompidou wanted to create a focus for modern art in the heart of Paris, in the old Les Halles district, which would be welcoming to all visitors, whatever their background. He also wanted Paris to regain its position of prominence in the international world of art.

The Musée National d'Art Moderne, which also attracts attention with its spectacular special exhibitions, is just one of the institutions housed in the Centre. It is also home to an important library and a museum of industrial design as well as the IRCAM (Institut de Recherche et Coordination

## CONTEMPORARY ART

The fourth floor is home to works from around 1960 to the present day. Due to new acquisitions, the structure and contents of the rooms tend to change more frequently than those displaying works of the 20th century. Jean Dubuffet, already represented on the fifth floor, is shown here once again in his own room with projects dating from 1968 to 1970: *Le Jardin d'Hiver*. A later work by Joseph Beuys, *Plight* (1985), also has its own room. Artists represented on this floor include Niki de Saint-Phalle, Jean Tinguely, Claes Oldenburg, Martial Raysse, Victor Vasarely, Wolf Vostell, and Cy Twombly, to name just a few of the best known.

It is not only art in its purest sense that is presented – space is also given to design, particularly the star French designer Philippe Starck, who has two rooms showing works such as *Lola Mundo* (1986, a chair), *Miss Sissi* (1991, a lamp), *Flambeau Olympique Albertville* (1992), *La Bohème* (2000, three vases). On this level there is also a new media room and a visitor salon, where you can find further information on the exhibited works.

## THE STUDIO OF CONSTANTIN BRANCUŞI

Located on the museum's forecourt where during the day and in the evening street artists, magicians, and buskers attract crowds of spectators, is the studio of the Romanian sculptor Constantin Brancuşi (1876–1957). It is housed in a special building on the side of the square facing the rue Rambuteau and forms a part of the museum. Constantin Brancuşi lived in Paris from 1904 until his death in 1957. From 1928, he worked in a studio at Montparnasse, which was demolished after his death and later replicated in the Centre Pompidou. In integrating the studio into the Musée National d'Art Moderne, Renzo Piano recreated its calm and secluded atmosphere, although the rooms have to remain open to visitors to the building.

You can also see his working materials, some of his tools, and more personal item such as written documents, pieces of furniture, and his books. His 160-volume library principally contains mainly titles on art, but his collection of records covers a very broad spectrum, with works by both classical composers and his contemporaries, such as Stravinsky and Satie, as well as folk and jazz. You can, of course, also see

# CENTRE POMPIDOU – MUSÉE NATIONAL D'ART MODERNE

Acoustique/Musique). Composer, Pierre Boulez is one of the founders of this institute and its first director. It is devoted to research in modern music and acoustics.

**The Stravinsky Fountain by Niki de Saint-Phalle and Jean Tinguely in front of the Centre Pompidou.**

some of his works in the three rooms of his studio, including *Sculpture pour Aveugles* (1920/21), *L'Oiseau dans l'Espace* (1923), *Colonne sans fin I* (1925), *Portrait de Nancy Cunard* (1928), *Grand Coq* (1930), and finally *Le Phoque* (1943–46).

Other exhibits include works by Daniel Burren, who caued a furore in 1986 with his installation of black and white, vertically striped columns in the courtyard of the Palais Royal. Now he is one of France's most respecred artists.

*Centre Pompidou (Musée National d'Art Moderne), place Georges Pompidou, Tel 44 78 12 33, www.centrepompidou.fr, Wed–Mon 11.00–21.00, Thurs to 23.00.*

**The Kiss**, 1922, by Constantin Brancuși.

Paris 233

The view from the Place de la Concorde across the Seine to the Palais Bourbon.

# CITY WALKS

However vast the French metropolis may appear at first sight, there are some districts where it is perfectly feasible to explore the city on foot. No visit to Paris would ever be complete without a stroll up and down the main boulevard of the city, the Champs-Élysées. The two islands in the river where the city's history began are also perfectly suited for walks and discoveries on foot. The same is true for the two old city districts on the left bank of the Seine; the Latin Quarter and the more peaceful Faubourg Saint-Germain; or simply glide along the Seine for a waterborne tour that relieves those tired legs.

# CITY WALKS

The futurist Glass Pyramid by Ieoh Ming Pei forms the main entrance to the Louvre.

## SIGHTS

### ❶ Notre-Dame

The construction of the fine Gothic cathedral of Notre-Dame began in 1163 and took over 150 years. Commissioned by bishop Paris Maurice de Sully, the interior dimensions of the cathedral are impressive: 130 m (426 ft) in length, 48 m (157 ft) wide and 35 m (114 ft) high. But despite its size, it has a sense of lightness and airiness, due in part to its magnificent stained-glass windows.

### ❷ Sainte-Chapelle

Originally the chapel of the royal palace of St Louis, Sainte-Chapelle is now incorporated into the Palais de Justice. It was originally commissioned by Louis IX to house holy relics, such as the Crown of Thorns. Sainte-Chapelle is famed for its delicate medieval stained-glass windows which date from the 12th to the 14th centuries and depict well-known Biblical scenes.

### ❸ Pont Neuf

The name of this beautiful bridge – New Bridge – is rather misleading. It is in fact the oldest bridge in Paris, completed in 1607. At 330 m (1,082 ft), it is also the longest in the city. The bridge has also served several times as a work of art – Christo wrapped it up in 1984, and the Japanese fashion designer Kenzo had it beautifully decked out in flowers.

### ❹ Louvre

This vast palace and former residence of French kings has been extended over the centuries and is today home to one of the most important art collections in the world. On your walk through the museum make sure you don't jut look at the paintings – the imposing and elegant building is a work of art in its own right

### ❺ Place Vendôme

Designed at the beginning of the 18th century by Jules Hardouin-Mansart, this large square features a delightful

236 Paris

# ÎLE DE LA CITÉ, RIVE DROITE

parade of buildings. Thanks to the jewelers such as Cartier and Cleef & Arpels it is the haunt of the rich and famous.

**❻ Opéra Garnier**
This lavish and ornate neo-baroque building was built to the designs by Charles Garnier between 1860 and 1875, during the reign of Napoleon III, finding a new style for his reign, the neo-baroque. Since the opening of the Opéra Bastille at the beginning of the 1990s, Opéra Garnier today no longer produces opera. Instead, ballet performances now take place here.

**❼ La Madeleine**
The church of La Madeleine was a long time in the planning: a domed baroque church

Paris 237

# CITY WALKS

Place de la Concorde, in the background the classicist façade of the church La Madeleine.

planned for the site during Louis XV's reign, then Louis XVI designed a classical building in the style of the Panthéon. But it was Napoleon Bonaparte who finally had plans drawn up to erect a temple to the glory of his great army, decorated with a series of Corinthian columns. The church was consecrated under King Louis-Philippe in 1842.

### ❽ Place de la Concorde
The largest square in Paris, and the second largest in France, has seen turbulent times. Originally a royal square, it was renamed the Place de la Révolution in 1792. It was here that the guillotine stood that ended the lives of Marie Antoinette and Louis XVI. After the upheavals ended, the square was given its current name as a sign of national reconciliation. The obelisk in the middle was a gift to France from the Egyptian vice-regent. The two fountains depict oceans and rivers; the female figures on the edge of the square symbolize the cities of Brest, Rouen, Lyon, Marseille, Bordeaux, Nantes, Strasbourg, and Lille.

### ❾ Champs-Élysées
The origins of this elegant and most French of avenues extending almost 2 km (2,187 yards) from the Place de la Concorde in the east to the Arc de Triomphe in the west, can be traced back to the second half of the 17th century. Most of the buildings that line the avenue were built in the 19th century. The wide pavements invite you to stroll and (window) shop.

### ❿ Arc de Triomphe
The foundation stone of this triumphal arch was laid under Napoleon in 1806, but the official opening did not take place until 1836. An eternal flame has been burning on the Tomb of the Unknown Soldier, beneath the arch, since 1923.

## SHOPPING

### ❶ Flower and bird markets
A wide range of pot-plants and cut flowers are on sale in this flower market, not far from Notre-Dame. On Sundays it is transformed into a bird market, selling parakeets, canaries, and all kinds of exotic birds.
*place Louis Lépine, 75004, Flower market: Tues–Sat 8.00–19.30, Bird Market: Sun 8.00–19.00, Métro Cité.*

### ❷ Hédiard
For over 150 years, Hédiard has been selling a wide range of produce of the highest quality, from sweet to savory.
*21 place de la Madeleine, 75008, Tel 43 12 88 88,*

# ÎLE DE LA CITÉ, RIVE DROITE

Evening on the Champs-Élysées and the end-of-work rush hour around the Arc de Triomphe.

*www.hediard.fr,*
*Mon–Sat 8.30–21.00,*
*Métro Madeleine.*

### 3 Pavillon Christofle

Everything on sale in this shop is in silver – from cutlery, tableware, and candlesticks to jewelry – in both modern and classic designs. This Parisian silversmith has a tradition stretching back to 1830.
*9 rue Royale, 75008,*
*Tel 55 27 99 13,*
*www.christofle.com,*
*Mon–Sat 9.00–19.30,*
*Métro Concorde.*

### 4 Virgin Megastore

A huge store offering a large selection of CDs, DVDs, books, and stationery. You can also buy tickets here for concerts and events in the city. And if you are hungry after shopping or strolling the length of the fabled Champs-Élysées, you can rest in the in-house café.
*52/60 avenue des Champs-Élysées, 75008, Tel 49 53 50 00,*
*www.virginmegastore.fr,*
*Mon–Sat 10.00–24.00, Sun 12.00–24.00, Métro George V.*

## EATING AND DRINKING

### 5 Taverne Henri IV

This small bistro, located not far from the statue of King Henri IV, at one end of the Île de la Cité, is popular with the lawyers from the nearby law courts of the Palais de Justice.
*13 place du Pont-Neuf, 75001, Tel 43 54 27 90,*
*Mon–Fri 11.30–21.30,*
*Sat 12.00–17.00,*
*Métro Pont-Neuf.*

### 6 Il Cortile

The restaurant of the Hôtel Castille, Il Cortile serves the best Italian cuisine. The dishes are inventive, and when the weather permits, food is also served on the pretty patio.
*37 rue Cambon, 75001,*
*Tel 44 58 44 17,*
*Mon–Fri 12.30–14.30, 19.30–22.30, Métro Madeleine.*

### 7 Senderens

Expensive and somewhat chilly in style, this (formerly the Lucas Carton) is one of the top restaurants in the city.
*9 place de la Madeleine, 75008, Tel 42 65 22 90,*
*www.senderens.fr,*
*12.00–14.45, 19.30–23.15, daily, Métro Madeleine.*

### 8 Ladurée

One of the best-known salons de thé in Paris. Ladurée also sells its own patisserie for breakfast, and serves full menus in the restaurant.
*75 avenue des Champs-Élysées, 75008,*
*Tel 40 75 08 75,*
*www.laduree.fr,*
*7.30–0.30, daily*
*Métro George V.*

# CITY WALKS

The windows of the Institut du Monde Arabe feature a decorative grid pattern.

## SIGHTS

### ❶ Institut du Monde Arabe

Founded in 1980 by France and 21 Arabic countries, this Arabic cultural institute houses a library, lecture halls, exhibition rooms, a cinema, a literary café, and a self-service restaurant in a building designed by a team of architects under the direction of Jean Nouvel and completed in 1987.

### ❷ Arènes de Lutèce

The remains of this ancient Roman arena from the first century were discovered in 1869, and are considered the oldest structure still in existence in Paris. Events are occasionally held here, and you can watch Parisians playing pétanque on the floor of the arena.

### ❸ Saint-Etienne-du-Mont

The most striking thing about this place of worship, constructed between 1492 and 1626 in a style that unites elements of Gothic and the Renaissance, is the magnificent choir screen flanked on both sides by richly decorated spiral staircases, created by Philibert de l'Orme. The philosopher Blaise Pascal and the dramatist Jean Racine are both buried in this church.

### ❹ Panthéon

Jacques-Germain Soufflot was commissioned by Louis XV to build a church for the glory of Saint Geneviève, the patron saint of Paris. Construction of the neoclassical edifice was completed in 1790, and in 1791 the Revolutionaries decided to convert the church into a Panthéon français. Famous citizens buried here include writers Victor Hugo and Alexandre Dumas, Émile Zola, the painter Jacques-Louis David, the philosophers Voltaire and Jean-Jacques Rousseau, the Resistance fighter Jean Moulin, and politicians Jean Jaurès and André Malraux.

### ❺ Sorbonne

This was the first university in Paris, and is also the oldest

240 Paris

# RIVE GAUCHE, QUARTIER LATIN

university in the whole of France. The roots of the Sorbonne can be traced back to the Middle Ages, when Robert de Sorbon, after whom it is named, founded a theological college. The university's current buildings in the Latin Quarter, on the Boulevard Saint-Michel and in the Place de la Sorbonne were constructed on the orders of Cardinal Richelieu, then rector of the university, in the first half of the 17th century. The Sorbonne continues to maintain its reputation as one of the world's most outstanding universities.

**⑥ Place de Furstenberg and Musée Delacroix**
Here, where the romantic, dreamy Place de Furstenberg

Paris 241

# CITY WALKS

The Jardin du Luxembourg is the perfect place to relax and swap some news and gossip.

lies in the shade of the plane trees, there was once the court of the abbey of Saint-Germain-des-Prés. At no. 6, the Musée Delacroix has been set up in the rooms where the painter Eugène Delacroix spent the last years of his life.

### ❼ Eglise Saint-Germain-des-Prés
This church is all that remains of one of the largest and richest Benedictine abbeys in Paris – the majority of the monastery buildings were destroyed in the Revolution. The present church dates back mainly to the 12th century; the wall paintings inside are 19th-century additions.

### ❽ Saint-Sulpice
The construction of the church of Saint-Sulpice took almost a century, from the mid-17th to the mid-18th century. Several architects were involved. The most striking element – the classical façade with its impressive rows of columns – was designed by the Italian architect Giovanni Niccolò Servandoni, who won the competiion to design and build the elaborate front.

### ❾ Jardin du Luxembourg
This park surrounding the Palais du Luxembourg, where the Senate now meets, is the green lung of the 5th and 6th arrondissements and provides generous space for many different leisure activities. For young visitors there is a marionette show, a carousel, and an adventure playground; for adults there are tennis courts, a place to play pétanque or chess, and also a pleasant café in which to enjoy the tranquilatmosphere. Beautiful sculptures by artists such as Jules Dalou are scattered around the park.

## SHOPPING

### ❶ Gibert Joseph
You will be spoiled for choice here – there is an overwhelming selection of books, DVDs, CDs, periodicals, and stationery available in this bookstore, the first branch of the Gibert Joseph chain, which was voted the best in France by the famousFrench literary magazine, *Livres Hebdo*.
*30 Boulevard Saint-Michel, 75006, Tel 44 41 88 86, www.gibertjoseph.com, Mon–Sat 10.00–19.30, Métro Cluny La Sorbonne.*

### ❷ Cacao et Chocolat
The name just says it all – this shop offers first-class chocolates, as well as delicious candies, truffles, chocolate coated nuts, and other delicacies made from cocoa. Try a hot chocolate at the bar or dip pieces of fruit into the

242 Paris

# RIVE GAUCHE, QUARTIER LATIN

The students' district, the Quartier Latin, is the location of Paris' foremost café: Le Procope.

chocolate fondue. An absolute must for anyone with a sweet tooth and gor all chocoholics, young and old!
*29 rue de Buci, 75006,*
*Tel 46 33 77 63,*
*www.cacaoetchocolat.com,*
*10.30–14.00, 15.00–19.30,*
*daily, Métro Mabillon.*

### 3 La Hune
This is an old-established Parisian art bookstore with a long tradition. Books on painting, sculpture, architecture, and photography.
*170 Boulevard Saint-Germain, 75006, Tel 45 48 35 85,*
*Mon–Sat 10.00–23.45,*
*Sun 11.00–19.45, Métro Saint-Germain-des-Prés.*

### 4 Yves Saint-Laurent
Sophisticated clothing from the famous fashion designer and inventor of prêt-à-porter fashion – who died in 2008 – for women who have plenty of money and appreciate the top-quality tailoring on offer.
*6 place Saint-Sulpice, 75006, Tel 43 29 43 00,*
*Mon 11.00–19.00, Tues–Sat 10.30–19.00, Métro Odéon.*

## EATING AND DRINKING

### 5 Le Cosi
Delicious Corsican cuisine, bringing a taste of the Mediterranean to the Latin Quarter. Many Corsican products are used in the various dishes, such as jams prepared by the chef's mother at home in Calvi.
*9 rue Cujas, 75005,*
*Tel 43 29 20 20,*
*www.paris-restaurant-cosi.com, Mon–Sat 12.00–14.30, from 19.30, Métro Cluny La Sorbonne.*

### 6 Bouillon Racine
Classic brasserie dishes are served at this restaurant. Guests dine in a beautiful room in an art deco building which dates from 1906.
*3 rue Racine, 75006*
*Tel 44 32 15 60,*
*www.bouillon-racine.com,*
*12.00–23.00, daily, Métro Cluny La Sorbonne.*

### 7 Le Procope
Today, the oldest café in Paris – founded in 1686 by the Italian Procopio dei Coltelli – is also a high-quality restaurant.
*13 rue de l'Ancienne Comédie, 75006, Tel 40 46 79 00,*
*www.procope.com, 10.30–1.00, daily, Métro Odéon.*

### 8 Kiwi Corner
Cuisine from Australia and New Zealand. Kangaroo fillet and exotic fish, plus wines.
*25 rue Servandoni, 75006,*
*Tel 46 33 12 06,*
*www.kiwicorner.fr,*
*Mon–Sat 12.00–15.00, from 19.00, Sun 12.00–15.30 (brunch), Métro Odéon.*

# CITY WALKS

Musée Rodin: The Thinker (1880) is one of the masterpieces of Auguste Rodin.

## SIGHTS

### ❶ Musée d'Orsay

Nineteenth-century works of art from several museums have been brought together in this former train station, originally built to coincide with the 1900 World Exhibition. Where noisy steam trains once departed, there is now a display of the world's most significant collection of art from this period to view, with the main focus on Impressionist and post-Impressionist paintings and sculpture.

### ❷ Palais Bourbon

The building in which the National Assembly – the French parliament – meets was originally a palace for a legitimized daughter of Louis XIV and his mistress Madame de Montespan. Napoleon added the classical portico in 1806 to mirror the Madeleine at the other end of the axis running from the Place de la Concorde to the Rue Royale.

### ❸ Musée Rodin

It is rare to find the works of an individual artist, even one as renowned as Rodin, displayed in such a splendid setting. The sculptor Auguste Rodin (1840–1917) lived in this bulding, also known as Hôtel Biron, from 1908 and spent the last years of his life here. Opened as a museum in 1919, it now displays inside the building and in the adjacent park his most famous sulptures, including *The Thinker*, *The Burghers of Calais*, *The Kiss*, *The Cathedral*, and *Balzac*.

### ❹ Hôtel and Dôme des Invalides

The Hôtel des Invalides was built between 1671 and 1676 on the orders of Louis XIV as a home for veterans of his wars. A church existed in this spot already, but the Sun King deemed it was too plain and so commissioned the Dôme des Invalides, built here in 1675, a magnificent domed edifice. Napoleon's sarcophagus lies inside the building directly

**244** Paris

# FAUBOURG SAINT-GERMAIN

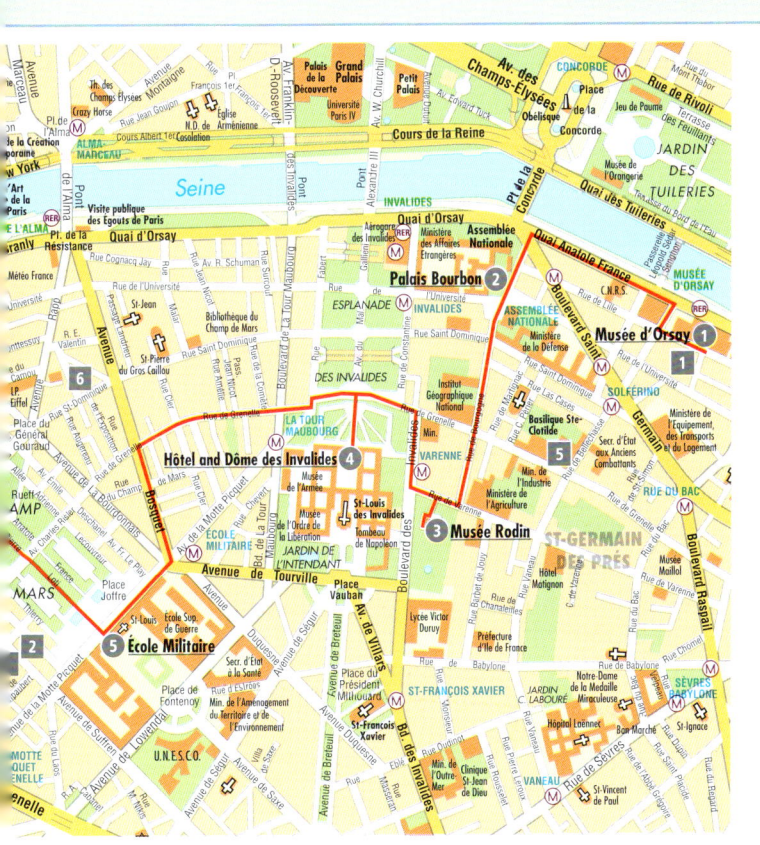

below the dome. Les Invalides houses several museums, including the French army's military museum.

### ❺ École Militaire

Louis XV had this military academy built by architect Ange-Jacques Gabriel at the instigation of his mistress Madame de Pompadour. Situated at the edge of the Champ-de-Mars, this building is considered to be one of the earliest examples of classicism in France. The academy opened in 1751, and one famous cadet who did part of his military training here in 1784, was Napoleon Bonaparte who graduated in just one year instead of the usual two. Officers are still trained for military service at the Academy.

Paris 245

# CITY WALKS

The bust of Gustave Eiffel can be seen at the foot of his most famous work, the Eiffel Tower.

### ❻ Eiffel Tower
It's hard to imagine today the indignation that was triggered by the construction of this wonderful filgree tower when it was erected for the World Exhibition in 1889. Built from around 10,000 tonnes (11, 023 UStons) of steel, there can be no other structure in the French capital that is as well known around the world as the 324-m-high (1,063-ft) tower designed by the enginee,r Gustave Eiffel. You can take a lift to its platforms, from where there is a fantastic view over the city and, in clear weather, far across to the Île-de-France.

### ❼ Palais de Chaillot
Constructed for the World Exhibition in 1937, the Palais de Chaillot now houses several museums and a playhouse. The generously proportioned building comprising two separate wings occupies an imposing position on an incline above the Seine, built on the foundations of the Palais Trocadéro. Its forecourt, with fountains and gilded figures, provides the best view of the Eiffel Tower – but watch out you don't get run over by enthusiastic skateboarders while taking your pictures.

### ❽ Palais Galliera
The palace was built in the 19th century for the Duchess of Galliera in the style of the neo-Renaissance. It is home to the Musée de la Mode et du Costume, which can only ever display a small selection of its 70,000 items dating from the 18th century to the present.

## SHOPPING

### ❶ Librairie 7L
Fashion, photography, and art are the prevailing themes in this ultra-cool bookshop owned by fashion designer Karl Lagerfeld. In addition to books, the shop stocks a wide selection of glossy international magazines.
*7 rue de Lille, 75007,*
*Tel 42 92 03 58,*
*Tues–Sat 10.30–19.00,*
*Métro Rue du Bac.*

### ❷ – ❹ Le Village Suisse
The following entries are all located in the Village Suisse, the collective name for more than a hundred antique shops and art galleries. The name "Swiss village" harks back to the Swiss pavilion at the World Exhibition in 1900.

### ❷ Galerie Alexandre
Pictures and sculptures from the 19th-20th centuries, with a focus on Russian art.
*78 avenue de Suffren, 75015,*
*Tel 40 56 93 77,*
*www.galeriealexandre.com,*

246 Paris

# FAUBOURG SAINT-GERMAIN

On a raised position above the Right Bank of the Seine, stands the Palais de Chaillot.

Thurs–Mon 11.00–19.00, Métro La Motte Piquet Grenelle.

### 3 Gislaine Chaplier
The ideal place to find a small and pretty, or unusual item to take home as a gift: thimbles, rattles, belt buckles, hatpins, safety pins and paper knives.
*10 avenue de Champaubert, 75015, Tel 46 67 30 55, www.ghislainechaplier.com, Thurs–Mon 11.00–13.00, 14.00–19.00, Métro La Motte-Piquet Grenelle.*

### 4 Vieileurop
An eclectic collection, ranging from paintings and sculpture, silverware and porcelain, to ancient 17th century weapons.
*75 Village Suisse, avenue de Champaubert, 75015, Tel 43 06 61 87, www.vieileurop.fr, Métro La Motte-Piquet Grenelle.*

## EATING AND DRINKING

### 5 Il Settimo
Salvatore Tassa, the owner of a restaurant in the outskirts of Rome, has now brought his native food to Paris.
*57 rue Bellechasse, 75007, Tel 45 50 39 27, Métro Solferino.*

### 6 Le Violon d'Ingres
Christian Constant offers a high standard of French cuisine, with exotic influences.
*135 rue Saint-Dominique, 75007, Tel 45 55 15 05, www.leviolondingres.com, Tues–Sat 12.00–14.30, 19.00–22.30, Métro La Tour-Maubourg.*

### 7 Altitude 95
For a great view of the Palais de Chaillot and the Seine, enjoy your meal at a height of around 95 m (311 ft) at one of the world's best-known and loved tourist attractions, the Eiffel Tower. The restaurant serves traditional French food in an elegant dining room.
*1st platform of the Eiffel Tower, 75007, Tel 08 25 56 66 62, www.restaurants-tour-eiffel.com, 12.00–14.00, 19.00–20.45, 21.00–23.15, daily, Métro Bir-Hakeim.*

### 8 La Table de Babette
This restaurant specializes in delicious and exotic Creole dishes, traditional fare from the Caribbean islands of the Antilles, prepared by Babette de Rozières, French celebrity TV chef and cookery teacher and well-known author of several best-selling cookbooks.
*32 rue de Longchamp, 75016, Tel 45 53 00 07, Mon–Fri 12.00–14.00, 19.15–22.30, Sat 19.15–23.00, Métro Iéna.*

# CITY WALKS

The statue of a Zouave soldier at the Pont de l'Alma.

SIGHTS

**❶ Pont de l'Alma**
Opened in 1856, this bridge was, for many years, used to assess water levels – when the Seine reached the feet of the statue of the Zouave soldier, the riverside quays were normally closed; in 1970 the statue was placed at a higher level. For many visitors, the bridge will always be linked with Princess Diana, who was fatally injured in the tunnel of the same name in August 1997.

**❷ Palais de Chaillot**
Built as an exhibition palace for the World Exhibition in 1937, the Palais de Chaillot is set on a hill above the Seine on the Right Bank. It houses several museums (Musée de la Marine, Musée de l'Homme,

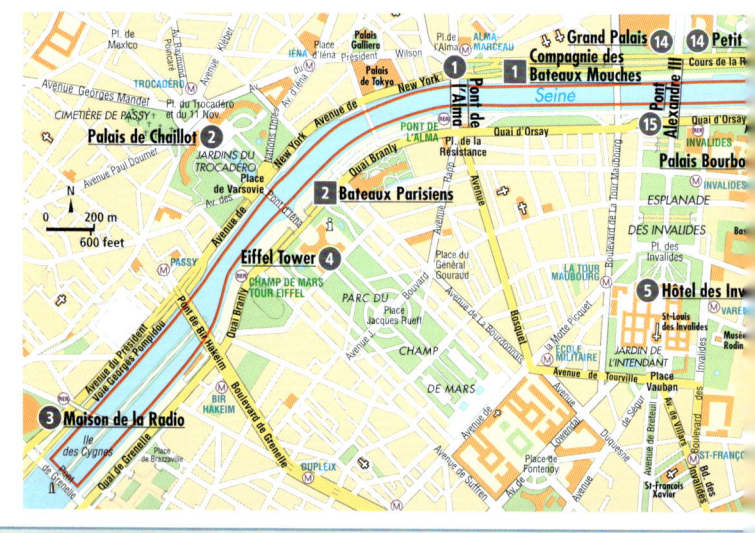

248 Paris

# SEINE CRUISE

A view of the circular building of the Maison de la Radio.

Musée des Monuments français) and the forecourt offers a pleasant place for relaxation and street performance.

❸ **Maison de la Radio**
Opened in 1963 and originally known as Maison de l'ORTF, the Maison de la Radio is today also known as Maison Ronde (Round House) because of its shape on plan – a circular structure of 500 m (1,640 ft) diameter around a tower block. In addition to broadcasting studios it also contains offices, a concert hall, and a museum devoted to the history of radio. The building had to be converted in 2003 because it no longer conformed to current fire safety regulations – and the construction work is set to continue until 2013.

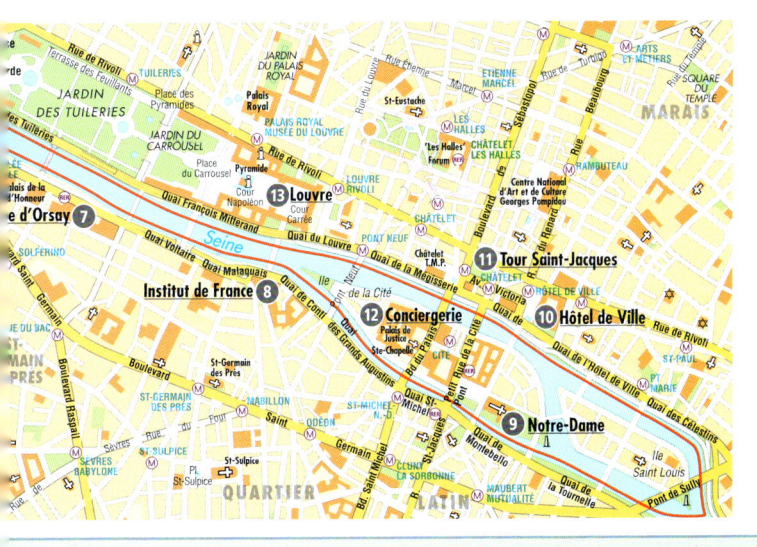

Paris 249

# CITY WALKS

*The view across the River Seine to the Cathedral of Notre-Dame.*

### ④ Eiffel Tower
No other building epitomizes Paris more than the Eiffel Tower. Erected as a provisional structure for the 1889 World Exhibition, it soon became a permanent fixture in the cityscape of the French capital. Today the filigree tower made from a special steel is one of the most visited attractions in France and Paris is unthinkable without it. There are three viewing platforms, the highest of which is at an altitude of 276 m (906 ft).

### ⑤ Hôtel des Invalides
On the southern bank of the Seine, the shining, leafgold-covered, 100-m-tall (328 ft) dome of the Hôtel des Invalides is a landmark, and visible from afar. More correctly called the Cathédrale Saint-Louis-des-Invalides, it acquired its more common name from its cupola (dôme).

### ⑥ Palais Bourbon
When the classical façade of the Palais Bourbon, the seat of the National Assembly, comes into view on the Left Bank, it is well worth glancing to the Right Bank to see its counterpart, the church of La Madeleine at the far end of the Place de la Concorde.

### ⑦ Musée d'Orsay
Built for the 1900 World Exhibition, the mighty structure of this former train station is hard to miss. The last train departed many years ago, but the building has a new role as a museum, containing a world-class collection of works of art from the 19th century.

### ⑧ Institut de France
The domed building was commissioned by Cardinal Richelieu and designed by Louis le Vau. It is now the seat of the – once royal – academies: the Académie Française – the most famous tasked with preserving the purity of the French language, the Académie des Beaux-Arts, the Académie des Inscriptions et Belles-Lettres, Académie des Sciences, and the Académie des Sciences Morales et Politiques.

### ⑨ Notre-Dame
This masterpiece of Gothic architecture, built between 1163 and 1345, rises in majestic splendor on the Île de la Cité. Its two towers with their flat rooftops and 90-m-tall (295-ft) crossing tower which reach toward heaven are unmistakable.

### ⑩ Hôtel de Ville
This building, dating from the 1870s, has housed the administrative offices for the City of Paris and the offices of the mayor since 1977. An earlier building was destroyed by the

# SEINE CRUISE

The Pont Alexandre III was named after the Russian czar, Alexander III.

opponents of the Paris Commune in 1871. The square in front of the building, formerly called La place de Grève, was the site of many executions.

**⑪ Tour Saint-Jacques**
In between the houses along the Seine banks, an impressive late-Gothic tower can be glimpsed. It is all that remains of the church of Saint-Jacques-la-Boucherie, which once was a starting point on the pilgrimage route to Santiago de Compostela in Spain.

**⑫ Conciergerie**
This structure creates an ambience of the Middle Ages in the heart of Paris on the Ile de la Cité. The oldest parts of this former royal palace and prison date back to the 14th century. The building gained notoriety in the Revolution, when many condemned prisoners awaited their execution here.

**⑬ Louvre**
The wings of the Louvre, which can be seen from the Seine, were built betwen the years 1546 and 1670 under the kings François I, Henri IV, Louis XIII, and Louis XIV. One section of the palace was significantly altered under Napoleon III. It is easy to glean the enormous size of the entire palace just from this section.

**⑭ Grand Palais, Petit Palais**
Both exhibition buildings were constructed for the World Exhibition of 1900. Their exterior is dominated by the domes and characterized by lavish neo-baroque details.

**⑮ Pont Alexandre III**
Paris's most magnificent bridge, completed in 1900, links the Esplanade des Invalides with the Avenue Winston Churchil, between Grand Palais and Petit Palais.

## TOUR COMPANIES

**1 Compagnie des Bateaux-Mouches**
In addition to basic tours, Bateaux Mouches also offer lunch (Sat, Sun and public holidays) or dinner cruises. Reservation is necessary.
*Port de la Conférence, Pont de l'Alma, Rive Droite, 75008, Tel 42 25 96 10, April–Sept 10.15, 11.00, 11.30, 12.15, 13.00, 13.45, 14.30, 15.15, 16.00–23 00 (every 20 mins), daily, Oct–March 10.15, 11.00, 12.15, 14.30, 16.00, 17.00, 18.00, 19.00, 20.00, 21.00, daily.*

**2 Bateaux Parisiens**
In addition to basic tours, there are lunch and/or dinner cruises and a tour for children.
*Port de la Bourdonnais, 75007, Tel 76 64 14 45, April–Sept 10.00–22.30, daily (every half hour), Oct–March every hour.*

Paris 251

## A
Accommodation see Hotels
Arc de Triomphe 24, 238
Arènes de Lutèce 240
Avenue de l'Opéra 57
Avenue Winston Churchill 29

## B
Bastille 78
Bateaux-Mouches, companies 251
Bateaux Parisiens, companies 251
Bibliothèque Nationale François Mitterrand (National Library) 166
Bois de Boulogne 144, 209
Boulevard Haussmann 40
Boulevard Raspail 116

## C
Canal Saint-Martin 158
Centre Pompidou 64, 230 f.
Champs-Élysées 24, 238
Montparnasse Cemetery 128
Cité de l'Architecture et du Patrimoine 32
Cité de la Musique 165
Cité des Sciences et de l'Industrie 165
Clubs/Bars
- Andy Wahloo 195
- Au Lapin Agile 211
- Le Mezzanine de l'Alcazar 203
- Wagg 203
Colonne de Juillet 76
Conciergerie 14, 251

## D
Disneyland Resort Paris 182, 213
Dôme des Invalides 124, 127, 244

## E
École Militaire 118, 245
Église Saint-Germain-des Prés 242
Eiffel Tower (Tour Eiffel) 132, 134, 246, 250
Élysée Palace 34

## F
Faubourg Saint-Germain 118 f.
Faubourg Saint-Honoré 34
Festivals and Events
- Fête des Tuileries 189
- Fête des Vendanges 209
- Foire Saint-Germain 197
- French Open 209
- Jazz à la Villette 209
- Paris Cinéma 197
- Paris Plages 189
- Tour de France, final stage 190
Fontainebleau 184
Forum des Halles 62
French Revolution 78 f.

## G
Galeries Lafayette 44
Gare d'Austerlitz 146
Gare de l'Est 146
Gare de Lyon 146
Gare du Nord 146
Gare Montparnasse 146
Gare Saint-Lazare 146
Goutte d'Or 117
Grand Palais 28, 251
Grande Arche 142, 148

## H
Hôtel Carnavalet 84
Hôtel de Cluny 222
Hôtel de Soubise 84
Hôtel de Ville 66, 250
Hôtel des Invalides 124, 244, 250
Hôtel Salé 82, 228
Hotels
- Amélie 207
- Comfort Hôtel Place du Tertre 211
- Ermitage Hôtel 211
- Grand Hôtel des Balcons 201
- Hôtel Aigle Noir, Fontainebleau 214
- Hôtel Caron de Beaumarchais 194
- Hôtel de l'Abbaye Saint-Germain 202
- Hôtel de la Bretonnerie 194
- Hôtel de Nesle 202
- Hôtel des Arts, Rueil Malmaison 214
- Hôtel des Deux-Îles 194
- Hôtel des Grandes Écoles 202
- Hôtel du Château, Vincennes 215
- Hôtel du Cygne 194
- Hôtel Eiffel Rive Gauche 207
- Hôtel la Bourdonnais 207

# INDEX

- Hôtel les Degrés de Notre-Dame 202
- Hôtel Lutetia 202
- Hôtel Madeleine-Opéra 195
- Hôtel Napoléon, Fontainebleau 215
- La Résidence du Berry, Versailles 215
- Murano Urban Resort 211
- Terrass Hôtel 211
- Trianon Palace, Versailles 215

I
Île de la Cité 11, 115 f.
Île des Cygnes 140
Île Saint-Louis 11, 115
Institut de France 91, 250
Institut du Monde Arabe 106, 240

J
Jardin du Luxembourg 102, 242
Jardins du Trocadéro 32
Jewish quarter 68

L
La Bagatelle 144
La Défense 142, 148
La Géode 165
La Madeleine 48, 237
Liberty Statue 141
Louvre 16 f., 168, 218 f., 236, 251

M
Maison de la Radio 248
Maison Européenne de la Photographie 188
Maison Nationale de l'Orangerie 188
Malmaison 178
Marais 68, 84
Marché aux Fleurs et aux Oiseaux (Flower and bird market) 116
Marché aux Puces (Flea market) 117
Marché Biologique 116
Métro 46
Montmartre 152, 156
Mosquée de Paris 106
Musée Carnavalet (Museummof the City of Paris) 85
Musée d'Art et d'Histoire, Saint-Denis 212
Musée d'Histoire Contemporaine 125
Musée d'Orsay 108, 111 f., 147, 244, 250
Musée de l'Armée 125
Musée de l'Éventail 208
Musée de l'Histoire de la France 85
Musée de l'Homme 33
Musée de l'Ordre de la Libération 125
Musée de la Curiosité et de la Magie 190
Musée de la Marine 32
Musée de la Poupée 190
Musée de Montmartre 208
Musée Delacroix 241

Musée des Arts et Métiers 86
Musée des Arts et Traditions (Ethnological Museum) 145
Musée des Carosses, Versailles 212
Musée des Égouts de Paris 204
Musée des Monuments Français 32
Musée des Plans et des Reliefs 125
Musée du Luxembourg 196
Musée du Quai Branly 136
Musée Édith Piaf 208
Musée en Herbe 209
Musée Maillol 204
Musée Marmottan Manet 110, 204
Musée National d'Art Moderne 230 f.
Musée National d'Histoire Naturelle 196
Musée National du Moyen Âge – Musée Cluny 222 f.
Musée National Picasso 82, 226 f.
Musée Rodin 122, 244
Musée Zadkine 196

N
Notre-Dame 12, 234, 236, 250

O
Opéra Bastille 56, 76, 168
Opéra Garnier 56, 237

P
Palais Bourbon 120, 244, 250

**Paris** 253

Palais de Chaillot 32, 246, 248
Palais de la Bourse 58
Palais de Tokyo 138
Palais du Luxembourg 104
Palais Galliera 246
Palais Royal 60
Panthéon 88, 98, 240
Parc de la Villette 164
Parc Zoologique de Paris, Vincennes 212
Père-Lachaise Cemetery 160
Petit Palais 28, 251
Place de Furstenberg 241
Place de la Bastille 76
Place de la Concorde 22, 238
Place de la Sorbonne 97
Place des Vosges 70
Place du Tertre 152
Place Vendôme 52, 236
Pont Alexandre III 28, 251
Pont de Bir-Hakeim 141
Pont de l'Alma 248
Pont Neuf 11, 236
Printemps 40

Q
Quartier Latin 88 f.

R
Restaurants/Cafés
 - Altitude 95 247
 - Au Boeuf Couronné 210
 - Au Pied de Cochon 192
 - Bouillon Racine 243
 - Café de la Paix 192
 - Café Marly 192
 - Fauchon 193
 - Globe Trotter Café 210
 - Hôtel du Nord 210
 - Huîtrerie Régis 200
 - Il Cortile 239
 - Il Settimo 247
 - Jardin Notre-Dame 200
 - Kiwi Corner 243
 - L'Ambroisie 71, 74, 193
 - L'Archipel, Vincennes 214
 - L'Atelier de Joël Robuchon 200
 - L'Étoile 207
 - La Bastide Odéon 200
 - La Brasserie de la Malmaison 214
 - La Crémaillère 152
 - La Marée de Versailles 213
 - La Table de Babette 247
 - La Tour d'Argent 200
 - Ladurée 239
 - Le Cosi 243
 - Le Jules Verne 206
 - Le Petit Bofinger 214
 - Le Potager du Père Thierry 210
 - Le Poulbot 210
 - Le Pré Catelan 74, 211
 - Le Procope 243
 - Le Souk 193
 - Le Train Bleu 147, 201
 - Le Violon d'Ingres 247
 - Le Ziryab 201
 - Les Deux Magots 91, 200
 - Maxim's 193
 - Senderens 239
 - Taverne Henri IV 239
 - Tokyo Eat 206
 - Zebra Square 206
 - Zen 194

Rue des Rosiers 68
Rue Mouffetard 117

S
Sacré-Coeur 150
Saint-Denis, Basilika von 180
Sainte-Chapelle 14, 236
Saint-Etienne-du-Mont 240
Saint-Germain-des Prés 90 f.
Saint-Sulpice 242
Seine 114
Seine Cruises
 see Bateaux-Mouches and Bateaux Parisiens
Shopping
 - Alain Mikli 205
 - Au Nain Bleu 191
 - Bazar de l'Hôtel de Ville 191
 - Boucheron 54
 - Bouquinistes 198
 - Cacao et Chocolat 242
 - Centre Commercial du Carrousel du Louvre 191
 - Chanel Joaillerie 191
 - Christoph Delcourt 210
 - Fauchon 50
 - Forum des Halles 62, 190
 - Galerie Alexandre 246
 - Galerie Véro-Dodat 192
 - Gibert Joseph 242
 - Gislaine Chaplier 247
 - Goutte d'Or 117
 - Hédiard 239
 - Hermès 192
 - L'Occitane en Provence 198
 - La Hune 243
 - Le Bon Marché 205
 - Le Village Suisse 246

254 Paris

# INDEX

- Librairie 7L 246
- Librairie des Enfants, Vincennes 213
- Marché aux Fleurs et aux Oiseaux (Flower and bird market) 116, 239
- Marché aux Puces (Flea market) 117
- Marché Biologique (Organic market) 116
- Mariage Frères 198
- Marie-Anne Cantin Fromagerie 205
- Pavillon Christofle 239
- Petit Bateau 199
- Potager du Roi, Versailles 213
- Rue Mouffetard 117
- Ryst Dupeyron 206
- Shakespeare & Company 199
- Skripta 199
- Sonia Rykiel 199
- Tati 210
- Vieileurop 247
- Virgin Megastore 239
- Yves Saint-Laurent 243

Sorbonne 96, 240

## T

Theaters/Concert halls/ Revues/Cinemas
- Cinéaqua 204
- Comédie Française 188
- Crazy Horse Saloon 195
- L'Élysée Montmartre 208
- L'Odéon – Théâtre de l'Europe 196
- La Pagode 207
- Le Cinéma du Panthéon 203
- Le Funambule de Montmartre 208
- Le Lido 195
- Les Marionettes du Champs-de-Mars 205
- Les Marionettes du Luxembourg 197
- Moulin Rouge 154, 211
- Olympia 95, 188
- Opéra Bastille 56, 168
- Opéra Garnier 56
- Studio des Ursulines 203
- Théâtre de la Huchette 197
- Théâtre de la Porte Saint-Martin 208
- Théâtre du Châtelet 189
- Théâtre du Palais Royal 189
- Théâtre du Soleil, Vincennes 212
- Théâtre du Vieux Colombier 197
- Théâtre National de Chaillot 204
- Théâtre National de Chaillot 33

Tour Saint-Jacques 251
Tuileries 20

## UV

Vaux-le-Vicomte 176
Versailles 172 f., 176

**Paris** 255

# PICTURE CREDITS/IMPRINT

A = Alamy  BB = Bilderberg  C = Corbis  G = Getty  L = laif  M = Mauritius

Front cover: A1Pix; back cover: L/Meyer; pp2/3: G/Barnes; pp4/5: G/Stirnberg, pp6/7: Premium; pp8/9: G/ Morandi; pp10/11t+b: A/David Giral; p11t: A/L. Zacharie; pp12/13: Bildagentur Huber; p13t: A/A1Pix; p13r: Caro/Sorge; pp14/15: Bilderberg/Dorothea Schmid; p15t: Schapowalow/SIME; p15r: Bilderberg; pp16/17: L/Meyer; p17 o: Premium; pp18/19: L/Galli; p19tl: bridgemanart.com; p19tc: akg-images; p19 r: bridgemanart.com; pp20/21: C/Woolfitt; p21t: C/Mellou; pp22/23: A/PCL; p23t: L/Hemis; pp24/25: L/REA; p25t: C/Sulgan; pp26/27: AKG/Album; p27tl: C/Christian Simonpietri; p27tc: Holger Andre; p27tr: C/Morgan Lecompte; p27t: akg-images/Films du Carosse; p27rb: akg-images; pp28/29: L/Krinitz; p29t: L/Meyer; p29r: Visum/Hoffmann; p30lt: bridgemanart.com; p30b: TV-yesterday; pp30/31: bridgemanart.com; p31t: bridgemanart.com; p32l: A/Kowalsky; p32/33: C/Simard; p33t: C/Nowitz; p34l: L/REA; pp34/35: L/Le Figaro; p35: Look/Johaentges, pp36/37 (all): bridgemanart.com; p38/39: G/Noton; p39t: C/Arthus-Bertrand; p39r: G/Vanderelst; pp40/41: Look/Pompe; p41t: Look/Pompe; p41r: A1Pix/JTB; p42l+c: C/Stephane Cardinale; p42r: C/EPA; p43t: C/Stephane Cardinale; p43l: C/EPA; p43c: C/Stephane Cardinale; p43r: L/UPI; p44l: C/Phototravel; pp44/45: L/Krinitz; p45t: C/Reuters; pp46/47: L/REA; p47r: A/Barnes; p47r: G/MacDougall; p48l: G/Cazin; pp48/49: C/Press; p49t: C/Karnow; pp50/51: G/Le Segretain; p51t: A/Directphoto; p51r: A/Horree; pp52/53: C/Simard; p53t +r: C/Seguin; pp56/57: C/Macduff Everton; p57t: L/Meyer; pp54/55: 55t +r: C/Sulgan; pp56/57: C/Macduff Everton; p57t: L/Meyer; pp56/57: L/Meyer; p57r: A/Mark Harmel; pp58/59: G/Segal; p59t: C/Godong; pp60/61: blickwinkel/Teister; p61t: Art Achive/Dagli Orti; pp62/63: G/Grandadam; p63t: bildstelle; pp64/65: L/Galli; p65t: G/Panoramic Images; p65l: all-five.de; pp66/67: C/Houser; p67t: C/Setboun; p67r: C/Simard; p68t: C/Gould, p68b: C/Holmes; pp68/69: C/Simard; p69t: C/Simard; pp70/71: C/Thevenart; p71t: L/Hemis; p71r: C/McConnachie; pp72/73: A/Kellerman; p73t: bridgemanart.com; p74l: C/Franken; pp74/75: C/Saget; p75t: C/Franken; pp76/77: C/Simard; p77t: NN; p77r: C/Simard; pp78/79 - p81r: bridgemanart.com; p82l: A/Kellermann; pp82/83: A/Kellermann; p83t: L/RAPHO; pp84/85: Bildagentur-online; p85t: A/Robert Fried; p85r: L/Meyer; pp86/87, 87t +r: A/Kellermann; pp88/89: C/Sebourn; S.90/91: A/Mediacolors; p91t: Mauritius/Profimedia; p91r: L/Hemis; p92l: L/Keystone France; pp92/93: bridgemanart.com; p93t: C/Hulton Deutsch Collection; pp94/95: C/David Lefranc; p95t: C/Amet Jean Pierre, p95r: C/Thierry Orban; pp96/97: A/Bogner; p97t: C/Setboun; p97r: L/Hemis; p98l: C/Holmes; S.98/99: L/Horst Dieter Zinn; p99t: A/Setboun; p100l+ 101t: bridgemanart.com; p101: Amary Evans Picture Library; p102: L/Hemis; pp102/103: A/Horwarth; p103t: A/Atlantide; pp104/105: C/Simard; p105t: C/Rowell; p105r: A1Pix/BIS; p106l: C/Fred De Noyelle/Godong; p106/107: L/Oddy; p107t: C/Forrestier; p108lt: L/Hemis/Ludovic Maisant; p108lb: L/Hemis; pp108/109: Bilderberg/Dorothea Schmid; p109t: L/hoa Qui; p110: A/Peter Horree; p111t: L/Keystone France; p111l: A/Peter Horree; p111r: A/The Printcollector; pp112/113 (all): A/Peter Horree; pp114/115: A/I.L Images; p115t: A/Viennaslide; p115r: C/Checurel; pp116/117: L/Hahn; p117t: C/Owen Franken; p117r: A/Tbkmedia; pp118/119: G/Cumming; pp120/121: G/Layma; p121t: A/Cole; p121r: akg-images/Laurent Lecat; pp122/123: A/Adam Eastland; p123t: alimdi.net; p123r: C/Christofori; p124l: A/Christophe Testi; pp124/125: G/Bibikow; p125t: A/JTB; pp126/127: A/Directphoto.org; p127t: bridgemanart.com; p127r: A/Classic Image; pp128/129: C/Heseltine; p129t: G/EyesWideOpen; p129r: G/EyesWideOpen; pp130/131t: G/Panoramic Images; pp130/131b: G/Panoramic Images; p131t: Look/Johaentges; p131r: G/Cunningham; pp132/133: L/Meyer; p133t: L/Meyer; p133r: Mauritius/Super Stock; pp134/135: Bilderberg/Dorothea Schmid; p135t (all three): bridgemanart.com; p135r: akg-images; p136l: L/Hemis/Rieger Bertrand; pp136/137: L/Hemis/Arnaud Chicurel; p137t: L/Hemis/Rieger Bertrand; p138l: L/Hemis/Ludovic Maisant; pp138/139: L/Cover; p139r: A/Raftery; p140l: C/Sulgan; pp140/141 + 141t: L/Meyer; pp142/143: L/Rees; pp144/145 (all): L/Hemis; pp146/147t +b: G/Panoramic Images; p147t: C/Simard; p147r: G/Panoramic Images; pp148/149: G/Lemoine; p149t: G/Koch; p149r: G/MacDougall; pp150/151: A/Yadav; p151t: C/Nowitz; p151r: C/Deloche; p152l: blickwinkel/McPhoto; pp152/153 + 153t: L/Hemis; p154/155: blickwinkel; p155t: blickwinkel; p155r: Look/Kreuzer; p155rb: Look/Kreuzer; pp156/157: Schapowalow/Robert Harding; p157tl+tr: A/Lordprice Collection; p157r: bridgemanart.com; pp158/159 + 159t: L/Meyer; p160l: L/Hemis; pp160/161: A/Matt Griggs; p161: A/Pictorial Press; pp162/163: L/RAPHO; p163t: akg-images; p163r: L/RAPHO; p164/165: Bildagentur Huber/G. Simeone; p165t: Huber/Simeone; pp166/167: C/Simard; p167t: akg-images/Catherine Bibollet; p167r: visum/Dangschat; p168l: C/Jean-Claude Amiel; pp168/169: L/Hoa-Qui; p169r: Huber/Stadler; pp170/171: Mauritius-images/age; 172lt, lb + 172/173: L/Hemis; p173t: laif; p214/14r: AKG; p175t: L/Hemis; p175l+r: AKG; p176l: bridgemanart.com; pp176/177: L/Hemis; p177t: L/Harpur Garden Library; pp178/179, 179t +r: akg-images/Laurent Lecat; pp180/181: L/Hemis; p181t: Mauritius-images/age; p181r: L/Hemis; pp182/183: Bilderberg/Bertold Steinhilber; p183t: A/Cubolmages; p183r: A/Smak; p184l: C/Ludovic Maisant; pp184/185: A/Jon Arnold Images; p185t: C/Ludovic Maisant; p186/187: A/Hollandse Hoogte; p188: L/Gallarde; p189: L/Maisant; p190: L/van Houtryve; p191: A/Alexandre; p192: L/Samson Thomas; p193: L/Jones; p194: Lonely Planet/Carillet; p195: Look/Kreuzer; p196: L/Hemis; p197: L/Rieger; p198: L/Hardy; p199: L/Krinitz; p200: L/Rougemont; p201: L/Fred; p202: M/Profimedia; p203: A/offiwent.com; p204: L/Sonnet; p205: L/Delalande; p206: L/Maisant; p207: L/Celentano; p208: Ernst Wrba; p209: L/Viot; p210: L/REA; p211: L/Droemens; pp212 + 213: L/Hemis; pp214: L/Escudero; p215: L/Sierpinski; pp216/217: L/Hemis; p219: L/Meyer; p219b - 225t: akg-images; p225b: Bilderberg/Modrak; p227t: Bilderberg/Peterschroeder; p227c: Bilderberg/Grames; p227b: Bilderberg/Grames; p229b: akg-images; p231t: L/RAPHO; p231b: akg-images; p233t: Uwe-Schmid; p233b: akg-images; pp234/235: L/TOP; p236: L/Galli; p238: L/Hemis; p239: L/Galli; p240: A/Neil Grant; p241: L/Hemis; p243: L/Sonnet; p244: L/Hemis; p246: L/Hoa-Qui; p247: C/Simard; p248 + 249: L/Hemis; p250: G/Morandi; L/Meyer.

© for the images on pp82/83, 226c+b, 229t+b: Succession Picasso/VG Bild-Kunst 2010, Bonn 2010, © for the images on p231b and 233b: VG Bild-Kunst, Bonn 2010

MONACO BOOKS is an imprint of Verlag Wolfgang Kunth
© Verlag Wolfgang Kunth GmbH & Co.KG, Munich, 2011
Concept: Wolfgang Kunth
Editing and design: Verlag Wolfgang Kunth GmbH&Co.KG
English translation/editing: Silva Editions Ltd.; JMS Books LLP

For distribution please contact:
Monaco Books
c/o Verlag Wolfgang Kunth, Königinstr.11
80539 München, Germany
Tel: +49 / 89/45 80 20 23
Fax: +49 / 89/ 45 80 20 21
info@kunth-verlag.de
www.monacobooks.com
www.kunth-verlag.de

All rights reserved. Reproduction, storage in a data processing system, or transmission by electronic means, by photocopying or similar, is only possible with the express permission of the copyright owner.

Printed in China

All facts have been researched with the greatest possible care to the best of our knowledge and belief. However, the editors and publishers can accept no responsibility for any inaccuracies or incompleteness of the details provided. The publishers are pleased to receive any information or suggestions for improvement.

# NOTES

# NOTES

# NOTES

# NOTES

# NOTES

# NOTES

# NOTES

# NOTES

# NOTES

# NOTES

# NOTES

# NOTES

# NOTES

# NOTES

# NOTES

# NOTES